# WOMEN AND SCHOOL LEADERSHIP

*International Perspectives*

*Edited by*

CECILIA REYNOLDS

STATE UNIVERSITY OF NEW YORK PRESS

Published by
STATE UNIVERSITY OF NEW YORK PRESS
ALBANY

© 2002  State University of New York

For information, address
State University of New York Press,
90 State Street, Suite 700, Albany, NY 12207

Production, Laurie Searl
Marketing, Jennifer Giovani


Library of Congress Cataloging-in-Publication Data

Women and school leadership : international perspectives / edited by Cecilia Reynolds.
    p.  cm. — (SUNY series in women in education)
Includes bibliographical references and index.
ISBN 0-7914-5311-1 (alk. paper) — ISBN 0-7914-5312-X (pbk. : alk. paper)
    1. Women school administrators—Cross-cultural studies. 2. Women college
administrators—Cross-cultural studies. 3. Educational leadership—Cross-cultural studies.
I. Reynolds, Cecilia, 1947– II. Series.

LB2831.8 .W64 2002
378.1'11'082—dc21
                                                                2001044660


10  9  8  7  6  5  4  3  2  1

# Contents

# ACKNOWLEDGMENTS

The completion of this book was made possible by a Connaught grant from the University of Toronto, for which I am most grateful.

The book would not have happened without the support of Margaret Grogan, the series editor, and the persistence and patience of all the chapter contributors. I also wish to acknowledge the editorial assistance of two graduate students, Deborah Mindorff and Robert White, who helped with various stages of the manuscript.

My sincere thanks to my husband Ted and my children Jennifer and James, who continue to accommodate the demands of my leadership work in education, including my work on this book.

INTRODUCTION

# NEW QUESTIONS ABOUT
# WOMEN AND SCHOOL LEADERSHIP

---

## Cecilia Reynolds

As we begin the twenty-first century, we hear more and more about trends toward globalization and about how our economies are driven by the vagaries of the global market (McQuaig 1998). We live in an era of rapid communication, and increasingly we find that people are reaching across international borders to tackle similar problems. Since the 1900s, in many countries around the globe, teaching has represented one of the largest occupational categories for women.[1] Despite a strong numerical representation in the teaching ranks, however, most often it has been men, not women, who have occupied official leadership roles in schools. The chapters in this book bring together international perspectives on women and school leadership and pose a number of questions designed to spark further inquiry about leadership, gender, and power in current school contexts in a number of countries.

In 1909, Ella Flagg Young, the first female superintendent of Chicago schools, optimistically declared that women were "destined to rule the schools of every city" (Blount 1998, 1). Her prediction was to fall sadly short, not only in America but also in countries such as Canada, Britain, New Zealand, and Australia. A number of important books and articles by several of the authors who have contributed to this volume (Blackmore and Kenway 1993 in Australia; Dunlap and Schmuck 1995 in the United States; Hall 1996 in the United Kingdom; Reynolds and Young 1995 in Canada; and Strachan 1997 in New Zealand) have addressed the issue of women and educational leadership through a feminist lens.

In 1998, I invited ten women from five different countries to participate in a symposium at the annual meeting of the American Educational Research

Association in San Diego, California. We came together to present information about our recent research on women and school leadership and to indicate questions that would enhance and enlarge existing discourse on this important topic. Along with our international audience, we began a debate at that symposium that challenged each of us to consider the differences and similarities in our perspectives and underlying assumptions. This book contains expanded versions of our symposium papers and brings together in one place ideas that, while developed in reference to particular localized settings, have implications for other venues. The collected works cross a number of borders and draw upon a rich interdisciplinary and international literature base.

    In the United States, organizational theorists Rosabeth Kanter (1977) and Kathy Ferguson (1984) and historians David Tyack and Elizabeth Hansot (1982), among others, have tried to explain the gendered division of labor in schools. In Canada, these themes have been explored by sociologists such as Dorothy Smith (1987) and by historians such as Alison Prentice (1977), who have pointed out that the development of publicly funded schools was largely accomplished because of a gendered division of labor whereby teaching, particularly of very young children, was viewed as most appropriately done by women (Danylewycz, Light, and Prentice 1987), while management, administration, and official leadership work, such as that done by the school superintendent, was seen as most appropriately "a man's task" (Abbott 1991). Economist Marilyn Waring (1989) in New Zealand and education critics such as Bob Connell (1987) from Australia, and Madeline Arnot (1986) and Gaby Weiner (1989) from Britain, to name only a few, also have offered important contributions to a vibrant, albeit muted, international discourse about the roles of men and women in elementary and secondary schools and in colleges and universities.

    The authors whose work is brought together in this book differ from one another in terms of their backgrounds, perspectives, writing styles, and research approaches. Clearly, despite these differences, they agree with Marcia Linn (1998) that much of the literature on women and educational leadership suggests

> an agenda for the future that sustains successful practices, while also broad-
> ening partnerships across disciplines, incorporating professional perspec-
> tives from other communities, and developing new methodologies for
> investigation. These perspectives . . . establish equity and diversity as
> respectable research, policy, and personal pursuits. (20)

    Several authors in this book discuss how difficult it has been for women to gain a "voice" within the dominant discourse on school leadership to speak about gender and its continuing importance in both theory and practice in education. Hall (chapter 1) and Young (chapter 4), in particular, discuss how many people, both males and females, operate on assumptions that policies and practices have changed for the better and that women are actually being advantaged now in their efforts to become school leaders and in their work to bring about gender equity in our schools at all levels. This book names that as a myth and provides international evidence to the contrary. It alerts the reader to the scope and complexity of the issues.

Presented here is an unprecedented compilation of current theories and perspectives on women and leadership issues in elementary, secondary, and postsecondary schools by several researchers who have gained stature in their own countries and internationally for their contributions to discourses about gender and school leadership. The About the Contributors section at the end of this book provides an overview of the breadth of their work. In her own way, each author has taken up the task of feminist deconstruction, that is,

> the feminist project of revealing the powerfully insistent hegemony of public discourse in maintaining hierarchy and inequality and of contesting identities ... and rewriting difference ... [as] part of the "habit change" or ways of thinking things differently within established ground. It emerges from those gaps endemic to all discourse, which are neither, stable, constant, nor absolute. (Luke 1990, .26)

Like the men and women they have studied, the authors illustrate "convergence and divergence of opinion," and their common interests in this topic "never serve to obliterate their individuality" (Kinnear 1995). They have used various methods to gather and analyze data, and they hold diverse theoretical positions. Coming from different countries, these women authors often use different spelling conventions and ways of speaking and writing. The authors work within "feminisms" rather than a single, easily classified version of feminist inquiry and theorizing. Like all research, the work presented here is not meant to be all-encompassing or to be the final word on the topic. On the contrary, the collection challenges the reader to consider both the partiality of all perspectives on leadership and future directions for research and practice.

Taken together, the chapters in this book present an international "state of the art" for research on women school leaders emanating from five selected nations where this topic has received some degree of currency and interest. This book should increase one's appreciation of the complexities of the tensions that people of both gender groups encounter as they accept and/or resist dominant models for school leaders. This book crosses international borders, but it also brings together views of schools and school systems at the macro level, with discussions and case studies focused on the micro level of school life. Local and global perspectives are connected and located in particular times and places. The authors avoid a romanticized progressivism that advocates an ever-improving situation with regard to issues concerning gender and leadership. Instead, they focus on the need for critical reflections that reveal hidden aspects of leadership phenomena. They advocate diverse forms of positive action to improve the situation for women in school settings.

The authors of the various chapters discuss a number of common themes. One such theme is the importance of historical context. Looking across differing contexts, the chapters illuminate patterns that persist and the ways in which change occurs. Organizational structures and contextual factors offer particular options or "scripts." Individual women and men make decisions regarding the taking up of available scripts within the teaching profession based on what they see as possible and desirable at a given time and place. Their decisions are not merely idiosyncratic and "free" choices, however. Economic, political, and social factors encourage certain choices over others, and thus leadership roles in schools can be viewed as highly "gendered," both in terms of who decides to take up the role and how they come to enact that role in a specific context.

Another common theme, almost the flip side to observations about gendered patterns of school leadership, is the claim that there is as much variation within gender groups as there is across gender groups. Taken as a whole, the chapters illustrate the multiplicity of individual responses observed when women leaders are the focus of inquiry. The authors consider how women are affected by the current educational climate, and they offer several suggestions for how we might proceed in the future, given what we know about the past and the present.

In various ways, the chapters speak to the positive results and unintended consequences of a feminist agenda for change in schools in several Western nations since the 1970s. While having participated in that feminist agenda in various ways themselves, the authors offer critical reflections about past efforts and suggest more fruitful paths for the future. One such path is the controversial area of "entrepreneurship" in schools and universities. What does it mean for men and women to take up school leadership in today's climate? This book is designed to enhance the international flavor of the reader's knowledge base in this area and may introduce the reader to new authors and perspectives.

## LIMITATIONS

The initial symposium and this book were limited by several pragmatic factors. It was not possible to be all-inclusive in terms of providing input from all of the persons who have made a substantial contribution to the field regarding the topic of women and leadership in education. Although the works here are somewhat representative of the bulk of the international literature base in English on this topic, many voices and perspectives are missing. Perhaps most obvious are limitations resulting from works from only five Western nations. The authors do not speak directly to the experiences of women throughout Europe, Asia, South America, Africa, the Middle East or to the wide variety of developing countries or those in Arctic regions or other parts of the globe. Much of what is written here, however, may indeed be applicable to those contexts or may spur questions concerning differences between women's experiences of school leadership within and across a variety of settings.

Also notable is the fact that all of the authors are white women currently working in an academic setting, which in itself situates them in certain sets of relations in terms of such factors as social class, race, ethnicity, and gender. Undercurrents can be found in many of the chapters regarding age, class, ethnicity, race, sexual orientation, physical abilities, and other aspects that often are confounding factors in terms of discussions of gender. These are frequently not highlighted in the general literature on women school leaders, and they are not highlighted in this book either. You will note, however, that many suggested questions for further study point to the importance of increasing our knowledge in these areas.

## FORMAT OF THE BOOK

This book is presented in a format designed to facilitate the identification of the main questions posed and discussed, as well as those raised for future study. I introduce each of the three sections and provide a list of suggested further readings at the end of the book.

## READERSHIP

Who will find this book of value? It is designed to speak to the interests of those studying and/or participating in educational leadership. It will be of particular interest to undergraduate or graduate students in the areas of women's studies, psychology, sociology, education, politics, or business. Many women and men who have taken on leadership roles may be curious about the experiences of leaders in school settings around the globe. They may wish to confirm their own interpretations of events and their reactions to them. They also may want to consider new perspectives or learn about theories that strive to explain connections between gender and leadership in various contexts. Thus the material here could provide an important form of personal and professional development, and it could help individuals formulate research questions that would move this area in fruitful new directions.

This book is relevant to both male and female readers, because it sheds light on the hidden role of gender in complex social structures and interactions in schools. Everyone concerned with social justice and equity issues can learn from the discourse on women school leaders. The December 1998 issue of the American journal *Educational Researcher* focused on affirmative action policy and the limited progress made in the United States and elsewhere with regard to gender equity. This book contributes to that discussion and adds the voices of women from around the world who have shared concerns about equity and how we might achieve it, given the current social climate within our school systems at all levels. The authors hope to encourage new directions for further inquiry and to impress upon the reader the urgency for continuing to ask new questions. This is crucial, since much of the current context, according to authors such as Linda McQuaig (1998), seems to encourage what she calls a "cult of impotence" that mitigates against hopeful action and leads instead to a resigned acceptance of the status quo.

## NOTE

1. A full discussion of women's movement into teaching as one of several gendered professional sectors in Western countries is provided by Kinnear (1995).

## REFERENCES

Abbott, J. 1991. "Accomplishing 'a Man's Task': Rural Women Teachers, Male Culture, and the School Inspectorate in Turn of the Century Ontario." *Gender and Education in Ontario*, ed. R. Heap and A. Prentice. Toronto: Canadian Scholars' Press.

Arnot, M. 1986. *Race, Gender, and Educational Policy Making.* Philadelphia: Module 4, Open University Press.

Blackmore, J., and J. Kenway, eds. 1993. *Gender Matters in Educational Administration and Policy: A Feminist Introduction.* Washington, D.C.: Falmer Press.

Blount, J. 1998. *Destined to Rule the Schools: Women and the Superintendency, 1873–1995.* Albany: State University of New York Press.

Connell, R.W. 1987. *Gender and Power.* Sydney: Allen & Unwin.

Danylewycz, M., B. Light, and A. Prentice. 1987. "The Evolution of the Sexual Division of Labor in Teaching: A Nineteenth Century Ontario and Quebec Case Study." *Women and Education*, ed. J. Gaskell and A. McClaren. Calgary: Detselig.

Dunlap, D., and P. Schmuck. 1995. *Women Leading in Education.* Albany: State University of New York Press.

Ferguson, K. 1984. *The Feminist Case against Bureaucracy.* Philadelphia: Temple University Press.

Hall, V. 1996. *Dancing on the Ceiling: A Study of Women Managers in Education.* London: Paul Chapman.

Kanter, R. 1977. *Men and Women of the Corporation.* New York: Basic Books.

Kinnear, M. 1995. *In Subordination: Professional Women, 1870–1970.* Montreal: McGill-Queen's University Press.

Linn, M. 1998. "When Good Intention and Subtle Stereotypes Clash: The Complexity of Selection Decision." *Educational Researcher* 27:9:15–17.

Luke, C., ed. 1998. *Feminisms and Pedagogies of Everyday Life.* Albany: State University of New York Press.

McQuaig, L. 1998. *The Cult of Impotence: Selling the Myth of Powerlessness in the Global Economy.* Toronto: Penguin Books.

Prentice, A. 1977. "The Feminization of Teaching." *The Neglected Majority,* ed. S. Trofimenkoff and A. Prentice. Toronto: McClelland & Stewart.

Reynolds, C., and B. Young, eds. 1995. *Women and Leadership in Canadian Education.* Calgary: Temeron Books.

Smith, D. 1987. *The Everyday World as Problematic: A Feminist Sociology.* Philadelphia: Open University Press.

Strachan, J. 1997. "Feminist Educational Leadership in a 'New Right' Context in Aotearoa, New Zealand." Unpublished Ph.D. thesis, University of Waikato.

Tyack, D., and E. Hansot. 1982. *Managers of Virtue: Public School Leadership in America, 1820–1980.* New York: Basic Books.

Waring, M. 1989. *Counting for Nothing: What Men Value and What Women Are Worth.* Sydney: Allen & Unwin.

Weiner, G. 1989. "Feminism, Equal Opportunities, and Vocationalism: The Changing Context." Pp. 107–121 in *Changing Perspectives on Gender: New Initiatives in Secondary Education,* ed. H. Burchell and V. Millman. Philadelphia: Open University Press.

# Part I

---

## Defining Shifting Contexts: Entrepreneurship, Changing Leadership Scripts, and the New Managerialism

The chapters of this book describe and analyze the position of women leaders in a variety of school settings and geographical contexts. In various ways, the authors question the status quo and how it came to be that way. They clarify what have come to be accepted truths about women and educational leadership, and they point out gaps in our current knowledge base.

In the first section of the book, ideas about entrepreneurship, leadership scripts, and the new managerialism are discussed with particular reference to the situation in Britain, Canada, and Australia. All three chapters stress the importance of historical context. These three chapters also claim that it is inaccurate to think that all women and all men respond to shifting contexts in the same way. Each author asks us to reconsider concepts and terminology commonly in use within the discourse about gender and educational leadership. We are asked to broaden our notions about the identities, moral dilemmas, and ways of leading that men and women have taken up in various contexts at different times and places.

In chapter 1, "Reinterpreting Entrepreneurship in Education: A Gender Perspective," Valerie Hall draws on her study of women "head-teachers" or principals in Britain in an era when entrepreneurship is a strong element of what Blackmore (chapter 3) has called the "new managerialism." Hall tells the story of her own journey into research on women school leaders and thus contextuates her questions about why feminist perspectives have had such a limited "impact on constructions of leading and managing in education." She also looks at contrasting interpretations of entrepreneurial activity in education, which on the one hand condemn it and on the other hand applaud it. Thus she picks up a theme regarding what authors in later chapters of this book call "transformational leadership."

Hall describes how her own study and other studies of women school leaders in Britain have found that few of them wish to be called feminists. She argues that while these women may not work to undermine patriarchal capitalism, their "individualistic enterprise" is an important area of study for those curious about women and leadership in schools and other organizations around the globe. Like all of the chapters in this book, Hall is interested in exploring "both structural features and the formation of professional identities." Like Reynolds (chapter 2), Hall posits the value of biographical data in order to integrate agency and structure in discussions of leadership as part of a person's career. Like Blackmore (chapter 3), Hall wishes to "move beyond the dualistic position which still remains embedded in feminist research in educational administration."

In this chapter, Hall describes how women lead and manage in two sectors, education and small business, to make the case that "it is possible to practice an alternative, ethical entrepreneurship." While she pulls from many studies within the United Kingdom, Hall also links her argument to work by researchers in Africa, Australia, Canada, and the United States. She discusses how careers of black teachers often reveal an emphasis on the promotion of racial justice, and she concludes that much of the literature on women leaders suggests that even though they may not consciously describe their work as being centered on the promotion of social justice, they do want "to retain their identities as leaders and managers."

Hall concludes this chapter by reminding us of the multiple ways in which women leaders can respond to conditions such as what she describes as "market place education" in Britain today. We have much to learn by examining women's "repertoire of management and leadership behaviors." Like Kenway and Langmead (chapter 7), Hall points out that as in elementary and secondary schools, in universities some women are actively transforming their organizations, others are coping, and still others are under severe stress. She reminds us of the value of what Kanter (1993) has called "quiet innovation," the translation of top-down strategies into actual practice in systems that both constrain and provide opportunity.

The next two chapters in this section employ feminist lenses to focus on women and fuse "experience and politics" (Mandell 1995) with regard to leadership within school settings. These chapters challenge how women and men see themselves and their social relationships. The researchers point out patterns in "gender scripts" from the past and the present, and they then extrapolate future trends based on their observations. Each author questions possible and desirable positions for women given shifts in the distribution of power in school organizations and the wider society over time.

In chapter 2, "Changing Gender Scripts and Moral Dilemmas for Women and Men in Education, 1940–1970," Cecilia Reynolds draws upon her life history study of two generations of men and women school principals in Ontario, Canada, to question changes in self-described moral dilemmas. In this chapter, Reynolds describes how feminist activities from the 1940s to the 1970s and changing economic and political circumstances can be said to have contributed to reconfigurations of the role of the school principal and changes in the latitude provided to men and women who take on that role.

Reynolds describes how early women "pioneers" who crossed over the gender line and took on principalships in the 1940s and 1950s in the Toronto Board of Education found themselves as outsiders in a masculinized cultural sphere. These women remembered being caught between a desire to remain feminine as a "dutiful daughter" and a wish to provide strong leadership and to bring about change. Women principals who took on the role in the same school board in the 1960s and 1970s did so in an era of employment equity policies advocated by feminist activists and designed to improve access for women to official leadership roles. Reynolds reports that these women frequently encountered backlash and anger directed toward them as women who were unwelcome newcomers to the school leadership game. They described dilemmas concerning feeling like tokens, dealing with gender stereotypes, and being perceived as unfair in dealing with girls and women in their schools.

Reynolds ends her chapter by advocating the importance of historical studies on men and women leaders. She suggests a number of areas that might prove fruitful and stresses the need to pay close attention to power dynamics in the society as well as within the organizations where women seek to increase their positions of power and influence.

In chapter 3, "Troubling Women: The Upsides and Downsides of Leadership and the New Managerialism," Jill Blackmore recognizes that women too frequently have been construed as "the trouble" in schools and in the labor force. Drawing on data from a large qualitative study of women leaders in Victoria, Australia, Kenway employs feminist perspectives to critique the discourses of "new managerialist" theory that calls for improved people management and stresses productivity. Like Kenway and Langmead (chapter 7), Blackmore draws conclusions about current trends in the Australian context, and she sees these as a threat not only to feminism and feminist teachers in universities but to the overall position of women in the society. Like Reynolds (chapter 2), Blackmore describes gender scripts available to women leaders in schools. She considers problems created for women leaders when they try to enact these gender scripts within the new managerialist context.

Blackmore provides a brief overview of the historical development of the new managerialism as a dominant discourse for postmodern management theory in an era of globalization. Within that discourse, efforts to deal with diversity and women, as part of the trouble that creates, have contributed to a renewed appeal for more women leaders. In many Western liberal capitalist states, the response to calls for equality has resulted only in a "regendering of work," so while more women have come to be accepted in some leadership roles, such as school principal, new barriers have actually blocked women from other leadership roles, such as the superintendency in a school system or a deanship in a university. In this chapter, Blackmore goes on to describe how calls for "women's ways of leading" have contributed to gender scripts for leaders, which serve to limit rather than expand possibilities for action.

According to Blackmore, women today may be seen "as trouble" in educational organizations, since they are currently striving for power and authority in a system that has historically denied this to them as a group, even though traditionally they have dominated the teaching profession in terms of numbers in many Western societies. Blackmore warns that women leaders may also be in trouble given today's circumstances with regard to schools and, once in leadership, they may be seen as "creating trouble," particularly if they attempt to break gender stereotypes. Women school leaders may also "trouble feminism itself." Blackmore illustrates how, despite its rich contribution, feminist literature on individual women leaders has led to a concentration on women as the problem in educational leadership "rather than problematizing the concept of leadership itself, relative to dominant power and gender relations." Indeed, as Blackmore points out, some feminists are troubled by the body of literature on women leaders which, they argue, is too focused on privileged, middle-class, white women.

Blackmore ends her chapter by mapping out five steps that she feels are strategically important for the future with regard to rethinking the discourse on women and school leadership. Her chapter, like the other two in Part 1, sets the stage for the remaining chapters, because it asks us to consider the various responses that individual women have had to similar circumstances. It presents an overview of some of the main facets of today's leadership climate in schools in most Western nations. These opening chapters also highlight the changing nature of contexts over time and the complexity of considering which questions might be most fruitful for future explorations and which questions would push the literature on this topic in new directions.

CHAPTER ONE


REINTERPRETING ENTREPRENEURSHIP IN EDUCATION:
A GENDER PERSPECTIVE


Valerie Hall
*United Kingdom*


INTRODUCTION

In this chapter, I have reflected on my own research and writing on educational management and gender in the context of the British education system. Like many of my contemporaries born toward the end of the Second World War, I have seen the ebb and flow of feminist theories as sources of explanations for different aspects of social life. I have been particularly struck by the failure of that theorizing to have any real impact on constructions of leading and managing in education. In different parts of the world, research continues to be reported that demonstrates the continuing absence of women from senior positions in public- and private-sector enterprises. My first question is, therefore, whether some feminist perspectives reinforce as well as challenge gender blindness by closing off options for both women and men to reposition themselves in relation to their own gender and sexual identities. The emphasis of much gender research on liberating leaders and managers may have undermined its potential to liberate management and leadership, whether done by men or women.

My second, not unconnected, question arises from the contrasting interpretations of entrepreneurial activity in education that lead on the one hand to condemnation and on the other hand to applause. For the critics, entrepreneurialism associated with managerialism is incompatible with education's moral purposes. Its aim is to replace a professional model of education with "a

largely discredited industrial management model" (Smyth 1993, 7). A counter-
argument might be made which, while not losing sight of the negative impact
of managerialism on education, reinterprets entrepreneurialism as a form of
creative management that is not necessarily incompatible with educational
goals. In its extreme version, the critical perspective would argue that one who
succeeds in the economy of schooling is inevitably seen to have failed as an
educator and a leader unless one's success has been combined with a challenge
to the system that frames one's management and leadership activities. Yet, I
would argue, recent research such as that by Osler (1997) on women and black
school principals (as members of groups likely to be still further marginalized
in new public-sector management as part of a bigger political project) shows
the possibilities of reinterpreting entrepreneurial activity in education in light
of research evidence about how women educators behave as managers and
leaders. How do other perspectives (of race, women's management and leadership activities outside of education, and developing as well as developed countries) combine with gender as a basis for reinterpreting entrepreneurship? What
do the voices of women who do not call themselves feminists tell us about
leading and managing in education?

These are intricate and risky questions as the following discussion shows,
but together they raise some thorny issues in a field that is dominated by concerns about women and leadership and critical theorists' concerns about education and management. What follows is an attempt to challenge some of the
ways in which these concerns and theories sometimes run the danger of closing down rather than opening up possibilities for women as leaders and managers in education.

## LEAVING HOME

My engagement with women's issues began in the early 1960s and has taken
many twists and turns. Now I am at a stage in my own use of feminist theorizing of what de Laurentis calls "leaving home." She describes this process as
"a displacement; leaving or giving up a place that is safe, that is home (physically, emotionally, linguistically, and epistemologically) for another place that is
unknown and risky" (quoted in Yeatman 1994, 49). In my case, it was a home
where I felt at times more a lodger than a full-time resident. The lessons I
learned in that home are, however, deeply imbedded and still provide a com-
pass for my continuing intellectual journey in this field. In part, the departure
from home was precipitated by the need (for career reasons) to engage with
management as a legitimate sphere of activity in education. This has meant
looking for its possibilities as well as its vices if I and colleagues are to support
those for whom it is a daily activity. Knowledge for understanding has to be
accompanied (though hopefully not contradicted) by knowledge for action.
While never losing a critical perspective (albeit in purist eyes, a somewhat tar-

nished one), understanding and working alongside those educational leaders have taken precedence over deconstructing the activities in which they are engaged. It seems important that our "expert" knowledge as analysts of education management should be accessible and helpful to those whose practices we are analyzing. Yeatman provides a satisfying justification for what might otherwise be seen as intellectual cowardice (i.e., jettisoning theory in favor of pragmatism) when she talks of feminist theory having matured to the point where it is able to subject its own premises to an ironical, skeptical, and critical mode of analysis (49). In this chapter I intend not only to subject my own feminist theorizing to such scrutiny but also my own and others' critical views of how some education leaders are responding to the demands of changing schools and colleges. Specific signposts on my journey to these questions (rather than their answers) have been my own recent research on women school principals as well as others' research into black women teachers and managers (Osler, 1997; Davidson, 1997), women principals in further education (Stott and Lawson 1997), and women in higher education (Deem and Ozga 1997), as well as my work with doctoral students in Britain, researching women's issues in their own countries. In this last group, in spite of a strong commitment to research inquiry into gender issues, many of my doctoral students remain very resistant to feminist theories that they do not see as relevant to the cultures with which they are concerned. In dialogue with these students, I am continually forced to question my own and others' theories of male hegemony not necessarily to reject them but to consider the ways they need reinterpreting. Davies and Gunawardena (1992) have demonstrated the need to identify how, for example, the locus of domestic responsibilities may be viewed differently. Looking at teachers in African and Far Eastern countries, they conclude, "The family occupies a central place for the orientations and ambitions of both sexes. It is not a predominantly female concern" (71).

In my recent research on women school leaders (Hall 1996) I coined the term *alternative entrepreneurs* to describe what I saw as their ethically based, proactive responses to managing schools in the new context of an educational marketplace (in England and Wales). This prompted further investigation of research and writing about women entrepreneurs outside of education that reveals a number of commonalities in their experiences and orientations. This investigation led me to my second question: Can entrepreneurial behavior as demonstrated by women be seen to represent a positive force in managing in education, or is it inevitably tarnished by its identification as the handmaiden of capitalism? As Goffee and Scase (1985) point out in their study of the experiences of female entrepreneurs, feminism rejects an interest in an area of activity (business ownership) that sustains an economic system that maintains the subordination of women to men. By implication, some feminists may also reject the accounts of women who lead in education but who do not overtly challenge patriarchy and managerialism. The tendency of much research into

women managers in education has been to focus on those who are declared
feminists (see, e.g., Adler, Laney, and Packer 1993; Deem and Ozga 1997;
Strachan 1997). Such women demonstrate a capacity to sustain an active commitment to changing processes and structures toward greater equity while
remaining buoyant in the choppy waters of education in the marketplace. Only
a few studies, such as that by Schmuck, Hollingsworth, and Lock in chapter 5,
have considered what happens when feminist women leaders "collide" with
their institutions.

Research in the context of England and Wales suggests that feminist
women leaders in education are thin on the ground. Coleman's national survey
of women head-teachers in England and Wales found that the majority assert-
ed that they did not make any distinction between men and women in terms
of providing support for professional development (Coleman 1998). Both my
own and Grace's (1995) study concluded that few women head-teachers were
prepared to declare themselves feminists. Goffee and Scase (1985) conclude
from their sample of female entrepreneurs that business start-up does not lead
to a fundamental reappraisal of the general position of women in society (98).
While both the "innovators" and "radicals" reject conventional female roles in
becoming entrepreneurs, the innovators "try to beat men at their own game,"
while the smaller number of radicals "try to carve out spheres of feminist
autonomy through collaboration and co-ownership" (117).

In contrast to studies of feminist education leaders, the intention of my
own research was to explore school leadership as practiced by six women, none
of whom described herself as a feminist. Rather, they demonstrated the same
fear of feminism that Grace (1995) identifies in his sample of women school
leaders: as an explicit social label that would identify them with unwelcome
stereotypes. Their self-distancing from the label, however, does not invalidate
what we can learn about education management and leadership from how they
do the job. They may fail the test of emancipatory praxis in the same way that
the literature on female entrepreneurs outside of education suggests is the case.
On the other hand, they demonstrate a way of managing and leading schools
which, although rooted in their own commitment to self-determination and
individual effort, is transformed by the purposes of education and cultures of
teaching. The values of the educators remain entwined with their purposes and
actions as managers. As Goffee and Scase (1985) remind us, the efforts of individual women in some African countries to achieve their economic independence from men through market trading (individualistic enterprise) can provide a basis for female solidarity (37).

With respect to women educational leaders in developed countries, I
would similarly argue that although their efforts may ultimately fail to undermine the institutions of patriarchal capitalism, such efforts make a powerful
contribution to children's and adults' learning. This, however, still begs the question of whether these women lead and manage in different ways from men.

From a critical perspective, the fact that women may appear to do it differently depends on how management and leadership are defined. Sinclair's (1998)
study of men and women senior executives in Australia shows that men frequently share much in common with their successful senior women colleagues.

## CHALLENGING GENDER MYOPIA

My first question referred to the danger of feminist theorizing obscuring rather
than illuminating our understanding of how women lead in education. The
problem with the more commonly used concept of overcoming gender blind-
ness is that it implies a one-way relationship in which those who cannot see are
shown the light by far-seeing feminists. Yet, however accurate feminist analyses
may be, they can tie and blind both ourselves (by imposing a theoretical strait-
jacket) and others who receive these messages like acid in the eye. In other
words, rigid feminist approaches can blinker, even though their purpose is to
remove blinkers that exist as a result of continuing taken-for-granted attitudes
to management as gender neutral. Those who have read widely in the field
(usually women, and still more usually, women academics) know that management is not gender neutral. But we are still a long way from convincing fellow
academics (men and women) and, more importantly, practitioners that management is a man-made enterprise. Gender myopia rather than gender blind-
ness offers the possibility of putting on new spectacles that reveal more clearly
what there is to be seen rather than invented (or theorized) in the unseeing
dark. An answer to my first question is framed by an assertion of the value of
theoretical and methodological perspectives that include gender for transforming the shadows of our understanding and bringing new or hitherto ignored
issues into the limelight. I choose gender rather than feminist to describe this
stance since, however sophisticated we may be as feminist theorists, we are, in
most countries, still ghosts at the education management feast.

In a national seminar series in England and Wales, which sought to redefine educational management, I was invited to contribute the gender perspective (through a written paper). In that paper (Hall 1999), in agreement with
Sinclair, I argue that as a manager, researcher, and teacher who is also a woman
I want to know what happens when men, as well as women, challenge the masculinist discourse. In another paper, reviewing gender as a theme in twenty-five
years of *Educational Management and Administration* (the journal of the British
Educational Management and Administration Society), I conclude that articles
with a gender perspective or theme continue only as a token presence with
minimal impact on the journal's dominant discourse (Hall 1997). The contribution of some male academics to the debate about gender (specifically men,
masculinities, and management—see Collinson and Hearn 1996) is a mixed
blessing in that it simultaneously legitimates the inquiry (particularly in the eyes
of other men) and highlights the inquiry's need for male legitimation.

How then can gender perspectives on leading and managing in education enlighten rather than blind? Like many other researchers who have a specific interest in gender, I have drawn on research methods that explore both
structural features and the formation of professional identities. Such approaches also take as axiomatic the need for researchers to situate themselves as men
and women who are managers, teachers, researchers, administrators, and politicians. Situating ourselves means recognizing the values that permeate the perspectives we take on these issues. As feminists, we are likely to have reflected
already on our stance toward the issues we are researching (although we may
not always rescrutinize that stance as frequently as we should). There is little
evidence that male researchers inquiring into managing and leading in education have asked themselves the same questions about their gender assumptions
relating to the topic. Stoll and Fink (1996, 111) suggest that effective school
leaders need to "invite themselves, physically, intellectually, socially, emotionally, spiritually" as a prelude to inviting others to working successfully for their
school. I would suggest that researchers also need to invite themselves in these
ways before they try to understand how others situate themselves in relation to
their own practice. Many studies have identified the importance of self-concept
for female managers (see, e.g. Davidson 1997; Hall 1996; Dillard 1995), but self-
concept is rarely explored in relation to men managers in education. An interesting exception (outside of education) is in Sinclair's (1998) study of senior
executives in Australia. In this study, she locates the possibility of doing leadership differently regarding both men's and women's capacity for self-examina-
tion and willingness to bring new and previously censored parts of themselves
into the workplace. Also relatively unexplored are the natural histories of educational leadership and the systematic ordering of biographical data that Gronn
(1996) identifies as the basis for ensuring the integration of agency and structure in a "leadership career framework." Gender approaches, such as those used
by many of the authors in this book, that are unfettered by overly determinis-
tic feminist theorizing can open up avenues of inquiry about and by both
women and men in this field.

## WOMEN AS ENTREPRENEURS IN EDUCATION

My second question addressed the possibility of reinterpreting entrepreneurship in the context of educational leadership, particularly as practiced by
women. To make the case that it is possible to practice an alternative, ethical
entrepreneurship in education, it is first necessary to review some arguments
for and against entrepreneurial approaches to leading and managing. Suggesting
that a particular type of entrepreneurialism might be seen as an acceptable positive approach in education does not mean denying the force of the critical
argument of the role of entrepreneurship in capitalism. Read's (1996) analysis
of the "self-made man" in Australian management links entrepreneurialism,

patriarchy, and masculinity in ways that appear to make any description of women as entrepreneurs impossible. In spite of acknowledging Goffee's and Scase's (1985) work, which shows how women in business act differently to their male counterparts, entrepreneurialism from Read's perspective remains firmly associated with economic efficiency and management control to the exclusion of all else. Yeatman (1994) and Deem and Ozga (1997) share similar views of the effects of the reorganization of universities as part of managed markets in which, according to Yeatman, "the academic leadership . . . is virtual putty in the government's hands" (43). Their and others' accounts paint a relatively gloomy picture of the possibilities for women managers in education for influencing positively effective learning environments.

This critical perspective condemns women's behavior as leaders and managers for being insufficiently emancipatory. It is certainly true in my study that, for the women head-teachers, being advocates for other disadvantaged individuals and groups, particularly women, took second place to their perceived need to preserve their own credibility and ensure the smooth running of the school. Their challenge to the perpetuation of male privilege came, in their view, from their presence and performance as school leaders. They demonstrated through their behavior that whatever they thought privately about gender differences and constraints on their performance as a result of being women, they were committed to a professionalism that took care not to discriminate against or in favor of men or women. Unlike the female entrepreneurs in other studies (see, e.g., Carter and Cannon 1988; Goffee and Scase 1985), they did not have as a primary motivation the desire to overcome experiences of subordination and blocked opportunities through business proprietorship, even though they took particular pride in the school (usually "our school," not "my school") for which they had ultimate responsibility as head-teachers. On the other hand, the motivation of many female entrepreneurs outside of education to overcome individual subordination is not shown to lead to collective challenges of the sources of subordination (other than the small group of radical female entrepreneurs in Goffee's and Scase's study).

There was no evidence in the women head-teachers study of them feeling that they and their teacher colleagues were being forced to set aside their own value systems to respond to the demands of a marketized system of education. As I argue later in this chapter, one explanation is that these women approached leading and managing schools in ways that protected teachers from feeling de-skilled and reinforced teachers' sense of professionalism. Critical perspectives on management would argue that managerial practices cannot be separated from particular masculinities that in turn "confirm the rights of management and men to manage" (Collinson and Hearn 1996, 11). Blackmore (1989) has convincingly argued that any apparent approbation of "feminine" characteristics for managers is merely a disguised form of appropriation of women's contribution to a masculine enterprise. However, I do not intend to justify an interpretation of women's behavior as educational managers and leaders mainly in terms of a response to critical perspectives. This would be falling into the same trap as arguments that describe women in terms of their differences from men; it implies a norm against which everything must be measured.

## THE POSSIBILITIES OF ENTREPRENEURIAL EDUCATORS

An alternative position with regard to studies about entrepreneurs and educational leadership might start from what is potentially good about entrepreneurialism and how it might be reinterpreted in education. My research suggested the possibility of being entrepreneurial in striving for the success (or even survival) of a school while simultaneously resisting governmental attempts to transform education into a form of business enterprise. The female heads' behavior demonstrated a model of educational entrepreneurialism that eschews managerialism in order to preserve the integrity of the educational enterprise and its ultimate goal: young people's learning and development. My claim that it eschews managerialism rests, not surprisingly perhaps, on how I saw the women leaders using power, managing staff, and transforming some of the externally generated reforms for the benefit of the school. What I observed resonated with Zeldin's (1995) discussion (in his *An Intimate History of Humanity*) of how managers are becoming intermediaries. He welcomes this new interpretation of the role of managers, exemplified, as he sees it, often through women's managerial behaviors. In his view, managers as intermediaries are catalysts who, recognizing the world as being in constant change, seek not to control it but to influence its direction. Tracing the role of leader through the centuries from dictator to intermediary, he notes in particular women's special contribution to its transformation. His conception of intermediaries, uniting insights from different kingdoms of knowledge, touches on my own proposal in *Dancing on the Ceiling* (Hall 1996) that women as managers may draw on extensive behavioral repertoires as a basis for leadership action. It is clear from the literature and from this study that women, unlike men, take both their mothers and their fathers as role models. This provides them with a broader range of behaviors or repertoire on which to base their own actions later in life (Hall 1996, 42). Zeldin quotes Maimonides' *Guide for the Perplexed* (a man writing in the thirteenth century) to exemplify the replacement of the power of force by the power of the imagination and new ways of seeing.

> Character consists of keeping out of the way of fools, not in conquering them . . . I see no honour for the victory of my soul. Even when men insult me I do not mind but answer politely with friendly words, or remain silent . . . I do not maintain that I never make mistakes. On the contrary, when I discover one, or if I am convinced of my error by others, I am ready to change everything in my writings, in my ways and even in my nature. (quoted in Zeldin 1995, 160)

Zeldin (1995) chooses the mayor of Strasbourg, Catherine Trautman, as his example of this new kind of intermediary. Influenced by her research on the Gnostics and their belief in transcending apparent opposites, including the differences between male and female, she identifies herself as a marginal integrated into society, intent on changing it from within.

> Women have been frightened by politics because they perceive it as a "hard" world; but in fact they have an advantage over men; women are "double-sided"; they view the world both as public and as private, which prevents them from getting lost in abstractions. Women have more freedom as politicians; men accept a lot of things from them that they won't tolerate from each other; and with women there is an expectation of new ideas, of change. (quoted in Zeldin 1995, 134)

All of these ideas can be viewed as examples of the appropriation of women's ways of being by continuing patriarchal forces, or they can be seen as alternative ways of representing the possibilities of leading and managing, drawing on a recognition of what women, as well as some men, bring to the process. The different research findings I have referred to so far all point to women managers and entrepreneurs describing a way of being, as a manager and a leader, which is not about compromised values and domination of others.

## ENTREPRENEURIALISM FOR WHAT?

The purpose of this next section is to identify similarities and differences between women managing and leading in two different sectors (education and small businesses) and to see to what extent they share values and behaviors. It draws on research findings relating to women in education management and women as entrepreneurs mainly in the United Kingdom. Women school leaders, it might be argued, have potentially two primary goals. The first is to run a successful school (i.e., one that provides an effective learning environment for young people). In this goal, they are no different from their male colleagues in education, although they do differ from women managers in other sectors where the ultimate goal is the profitability of the organization. The second goal is measured by the success of the children. Although women managers outside of education are usually discussed and describe themselves in terms of their "career success" (White, Cox, and Cooper 1992), the women school leaders in my study described their success in terms of the success of young people in their school.

### SIMILARITIES

Interestingly, for the women educational leaders I studied in the United Kingdom, the satisfactions of the job appeared to outweigh the stresses, in spite of the heavy stress levels reported for male head teachers in the United Kingdom, reflected in an increasing number of departures from the profession. My title *Dancing on the Ceiling* was intended to capture women's satisfaction in leading, rather than following, and in shaping the school for success. In this satisfaction of being in charge, they resembled the female entrepreneurs in Carter's and Cannon's (1988) study of women entrepreneurs, the black women headteachers in Osler (1997), and the women principals in further education colleges (Stott and Lawson 1997). All three groups, however, differ from the women managers described in Davidson's (1997) and Marshall's (1995) studies of women managers outside of education. In these last two studies, levels of occupational stress were high as a result of discrimination and prejudice. Davidson calls this "the gender factor" (67). Women in Marshall's study felt powerless to change the workplace cultures of which they were a part and decided to "move on." The theme of women exiting administrative positions is discussed in more detail in chapter 5 of this book.

## DIFFERENCES

The main difference between the women leaders in education and women entrepreneurs in small businesses was in the motivation that led them to their leading positions. The women entrepreneurs in Carter's and Cannon's study were driven by the desire to achieve an independence that was interpreted differently within different age groups. For the high-achieving women entrepreneurs in business (who most closely resemble women school leaders in other respects), a primary motivation was to overcome gender-related career blocks. This was not the case for the women school leaders for whom the desire "to make things happen" in their schools was uppermost. The common denominator between women managers and leaders within and between the different groups was, however, the wish for self-realization through their own enterprise. This raises interesting issues about the making of managers in different occupational sectors and different cultures. It challenges the legitimacy of adopting a single theory that explains management as masculine.

## SHARED VALUES AND BELIEFS

The second more controversial goal of women school leaders relates to the extent of their commitment to emancipatory praxis. The goal is not exclusively associated with women, but the expectation is higher and more frequently expressed as a result of what are assumed to be their own experiences, as women, of the effects of gender inequality. In holding up a mirror to women's performances as educational leaders, we hope to see reflected actions that support equality in all of its forms. Strachan, in chapter 6 of this book, provides examples of some of the different forms that women's leadership can take. The same mirror is less frequently held up to men as educational leaders (other than by those with an explicitly critical approach [see, e.g., Southworth 1995]). When the mirror fails to reveal a commitment to this second goal, respect for how women educational leaders work to achieve the first is often undermined. The argument is then made that a school's success can and should only be measured in terms of its ability to provide social justice for all of its students and staff. Yet the literature on women entrepreneurs and successful women in other sectors does not deem failure to achieve the second goal as an indictment of performance to achieve the first. The issue is whether, in an educational age driven by the values of the marketplace, school leaders fighting for the success of their schools (and using all of their creative skills as innovators to do so) are necessarily replacing the ethical purposes of education with the commercial values of business and industry.

Both of these goals (of achieving school or college success and emancipatory praxis) assume agency on the part of the manager or leader, but that agency may take a different form for the second goal than for the first. Marshall (1984), in her discussion of women managers as travelers in a male world, distinguishes between agency as masculine and communion as feminine. There is no guarantee that, even if they are combined, action directed toward greater social justice will emerge. Even "good intentions" on the part of managers and leaders are questionable, Yeatman (1994, 7) claims, unless managers challenge the dominant discourse. By implication, using this perspective, a black school leader fails unless he or she acts in the direct interests of black students and staff, and a woman school leader fails unless she works in the interests of other girls and women. Yet managers may be, in their own terms, acting in the interests of equity for all, through their attempts to achieve their goal of school or college success.

Osler's (1997) account of the education and careers of black teachers (men and women) concludes that they share an overall aim, the promotion of racial justice. For them, management is a largely political activity through which they seek to direct their power to promote particular goals (135). They have a vision of education that has developed out of their experience of disadvantage and discrimination. For black women school leaders that disadvantage is two-headed, as other literature confirms (see, e.g., Davidson 1997; Walker 1993). But their responses to the felt need to fight for social justice may be more ambivalent than Osler's conclusion suggests. As Osler points out, they may be seen by some as "professional ethnics," expert only in matters of race (135). This, some admit, constrains their actions, particularly if they are seeking career success. In her typology of responses to racism in education, she identifies senior educators with the "challenging" position. She also points out the difficulties of that position for senior black educators who perceive themselves to be particularly visible and vulnerable to hostile press reaction for behaviors that might go unnoticed in a white senior educator (196).

Whatever the constraints, the commitment to social justice of the senior black educators in Osler's study shines through (though she does not address whether it encompasses gender as well as race). More commonly in the accounts of the work of mainly white senior women educators, fighting to meet the first goal of running an effective school takes priority. All of the studies of women in management referred to so far, both in and outside of education, have in common an interest in the problems that women face in addition to, or different from, those faced by men in similar positions. While only rarely avowedly feminist, women school leaders seem to be conscious of needing to retain their identities as leaders and managers. In *Dancing on the Ceiling*, I expressed this in terms of the contradictory norms influencing interaction with women as school leaders. The ways in which these women managed their own behavior reflected continual minute adjustments to match their own and others' perceptions of them as women in a leadership role. Many of these adjustments were aimed at securing respect as a foundation for working with others in order to achieve mutual goals.

Zeldin's (1995) discussion of new ways forward for humanity argues for respect being more desirable than power. He associates respect with some women's ways of using power, acting not as chiefs but as "mediators, arbitrators, encouragers, and counsellors," or what the Icelandic sagas call "peaceweavers" (144). The problem, as he acknowledges, is that skilled manipulators of power can only be dislodged by other skilled manipulators of power. In spite of this, my own and other studies find commonalities in women leaders' determination to be "wise politicians"; that is, shrewd readers of the politics of organizations who combine action choices with integrity (Hall 1996, 159).

It has become almost axiomatic that women leaders use power differently from most men leaders, though I would argue that these differences arise from socialization and contextual factors rather than essentially different qualities. Stott and Lawson (1997) list the guiding principles of women leaders of further education colleges in the United Kingdom. They include: valuing and motivating; team working and shared decision making; listening; students coming first; accountability, honesty and integrity; equality of opportunity and empowerment; commitment to community; commitment to staff; being a reflective manager; and staff development. Few studies of women managers and leaders would contradict this list. Unfortunately, we have less evidence of what these and other principles look like in action, since observational data collection in this area still lags way behind interview data. As a result, it is still too easy for men, as well as for some women, to claim these qualities and still practice heroic leadership, thereby casting doubt on the whole enterprise of viewing leadership differently.

## ENTREPRENEURSHIP: THE EDUCATOR'S COMPROMISE?

Although I have claimed that the leadership styles of many women school leaders in different education systems appear to be characterized by principles of integrity and honesty, others would argue that the conditions of marketplace education inevitably compromise their application or make them appear naive. Elsewhere I have argued with Elliott, that managing staff in higher education has placed leaders in this setting in a context in which predominantly business orientations are beginning to dominate (Elliott and Hall 1994). Evetts (1990) has similarly argued that the changes brought about by the 1988 Reform Act in the United Kingdom require managerialist approaches that present cultural dilemmas for women head-teachers, particularly in elementary schools. At the same time, women have been shown in my own study as responding proactively to the opportunities these reforms bring to take the school forward. Somehow, some women school leaders are managing to combine the principles of service with the new business requirements of educational institutions.

In higher education, however, women's attempts to transform new requirements into positive learning outcomes for students appear as a losing battle, as illustrated in chapters 5 and 6 of this book. Why does this appear to be so? Are there other factors involved outside of those related to management techniques? The higher profile of gender awareness and the constraints imposed on women in academia may come from the nature of the work. Contact with stakeholders in higher education settings may be more variable than in elementary and secondary schools (in the United Kingdom at least), since universities are more isolated from the communities they serve and, internally, staff are more isolated from other colleagues (see Kenway and Langmead's discussion of this in chapter 7 of this book). On the other hand, Deem and Ozga (1997) rightly warn against the danger of interpreting others' accounts in ways that may not be acceptable to them. They acknowledge that in their sample they found women, including women in academia, who are in the act of transforming their organizations and are coping, though they are stressed (36). Their critical perspective warns against accepting apparent connections between women's strengths as managers and their advocated new ways of managing. The connections may become "ties that bind the women managers to their institutions, thereby contributing to the surface amelioration of the unacceptable" (37).

This critique and what I have described as the failure of many women educational leaders to make issues of social justice a priority would appear to negate my claim that we can identify a new or an alternative form of entrepreneurialism in education demonstrated in women's leadership styles. Yet I have shown in this chapter the many ways in which research suggests that women school leaders do try to change the educational dance they lead. Reading studies of women school leaders in New Zealand (Court 1994; Strachan 1997), in Canada (Reynolds and Young 1995), and in the United States (Dunlap and Schmuck 1995), as well as those I have mentioned from the United Kingdom, the same messages keep surfacing. However critical our perspective on women leaders and managers in education, these women are getting on with the job in ways that contribute to quality education. Their work is also bringing them personal and professional satisfaction. Perhaps the answer is in acknowledging that it is not entrepreneurialism itself that is wrong but in whose and what interests it is practiced. In the education systems described here, while strategy may be set from the top, women education leaders and managers, like other women entrepreneurs, can determine the meaning of change. There is considerable evidence of women's capacity to harness the talents of those with whom they work. Kanter (1993) talks of corporate entrepreneurs who are

> often the authors not of the grand gesture but of the quiet innovation. They are the ones who translate strategy—set at the top—into actual practice, and by doing so, shape what that strategy turns out to mean. (354)

Women's capabilities as innovators are not necessarily superior to men's, but our analyses of the ways in which women learn to act in "masculine" environments show that many have evolved a repertoire of management and leadership behaviors that works to the ethical as well as to the social benefit of education. Even if they fall short of emancipatory praxis, we can learn from such practices and view them as approaches that achieve the goal of creating schools in which young people learn well. The women head-teachers in my study interpreted their professional stance as one that should not distinguish between men and women. This was their conception of equity, and they extended this conception to encompass the children in their care. In order to move toward an alternative form of leadership in education that is both ethical and effective, we need to take account of the positive lessons we learn from women in these positions. We also need to consider how they can be combined with a greater awareness of what is needed to create social justice while remaining in the systems that provide both constraints and opportunities.

## REFERENCES

Adler, S., J. Laney, and M. Packer. 1993. *Managing Women: Feminism and Power in Educational Management.* Philadelphia: Open University Press.

Blackmore, J. 1989. "Educational Leadership: A Feminist Critique and Reconstruction." Pp. 93–129 in *Critical Perspectives on Educational Leadership,* ed. J. Smyth. London: Falmer Press.

Carter, S., and T. Cannon. 1988. *Female Entrepreneurs—A Study of Female Business Owners; Their Motivations, Experiences, and Strategies for Success.* London: HMSO.

Coleman, M. 1998. *Women in Education Management: The Career Progress and Leadership Styles of Female Secondary Headteachers in England and Wales.* Unpublished Ph.D. thesis, University of Leicester, England.

Collinson, D., and J. Hearn, eds. 1996. *Men As Managers, Managers As Men: Critical Perspectives on Men, Masculinities, and Management.* London: Sage Publications.

Court, M. 1994. *Women Transforming Leadership*. Palmerston North: ERDC Press.

Davidson, M. J. 1997. *The Black and Ethnic Minority Woman Manager: Cracking the Concrete Ceiling*. London: Paul Chapman.

Davies, L., and C. Gunawardena. 1992. *Women and Men in Educational Management: An International Inquiry*. IIEP Research Report No. 95. Paris: International Institute for Educational Planning.

Deem, R., and J. Ozga. 1997. "Women Managing for Diversity in a Postmodern World." Pp. 25–40 in *Feminist Critical Policy Analysis: A Perspective from Post-Secondary Education*, ed. C. Marshall. London: Falmer Press.

Dillard, C. B. 1995. Leading with Her Life: An African American (Re)interpretation of Leadership for an Urban High School Principal. *Educational Administration Quarterly* 31:4:539–63.

Dunlap, D., and P. Schmuck, eds. 1995. *Women Leading in Education*. Albany: State University of New York Press.

Elliott, G., and V. Hall. 1994. "FE Inc—Business Orientation in Further Education and the Introduction of Human Resource Management." *School Organization* 14:1:3–10.

Evetts, J. 1990. *Women in Primary Teaching: Career Contexts and Strategies*. London: Unwin Hyman.

Goffee, R., and R. Scase. 1985. *Women in Charge: The Experiences of Female Entrepreneurs*. London: Allen & Unwin.

Grace, G. 1995. *School Leadership: Beyond Education Management: An Essay in Policy Sholarship*. London: Falmer Press.

Gronn, P. 1996. "From Transactions to Transformations—A New World Order in the Study of Leadership?" *Educational Administration Quarterly* 24:1:7–30.

Hall, V. 1996. *Dancing on the Ceiling*. London: Paul Chapman.

Hall, V. 1997. "Dusting Off the Phoenix: Gender and Educational Leadership Revisited." *Educational Management and Administration* 25:3 (July): 309–24.

Hall, V. 1999. "Gender and Education Management: Duel or Dialogue." Pp. 155–65 in *Educational Management: Redefining Theory, Policy and Practice*, ed. T. Bush et al. London: Chapman.

Kanter, R. M. 1993. *The Change Masters: Corporate Entrepreneurs at Work*. London: Unwin.

Marshall, J. 1984. *Women Managers: Travellers in a Male World*. Chichester: Wiley.

Marshall, J. 1995. *Women Managers Moving On: Exploring Career and Life Choices*. Chichester: Wiley.

Osler, A. 1997. *The Education and Careers of Black Teachers: Changing Identities, Changing Lives*. Buckingham: Open University Press.

Read, R. 1996. "Entrepreneurialism and Paternalism in Australian Management: A Gender Critique of the 'Self-made' Man." Pp. 99–122 in *Collinson 1996*.

Reynolds, C., and B. Young, eds. 1995. *Women and Leadership in Canadian Education*. Calgary: Temeron Books.

Sinclair, A. 1998. *Doing Leadership Differently: Gender, Power, and Sexuality in a Changing Business Culture.* Victoria, Australia: Melbourne University Press.

Smyth, J., ed. 1993. *A Socially Critical View of the Self-Managing School.* London: Falmer Press.

Southworth, G. 1995. *Looking into Primary Headship: A Research Based Interpretation.* London: Falmer Press.

Stoll, L., and D. Fink. 1996. *Changing Our Schools.* Buckingham: Open University Press.

Stott, C., and L. Lawson. 1997. *Women at the Top in Further Education.* London: FEDA Report.

Strachan, J. 1997. "Feminist Educational Leadership in a 'New Right' Context in Aotearoa/New Zealand." Unpublished Ph.D. thesis, University of Waikato.

Walker, C. 1993. "Black Women in Educational Management." Pp. 16–24 in *Women in Educational Management*, ed. J. Ozga. Buckingham: Open University Press.

White, B., C. Cox, and C. Cooper. 1992. *Women's Career Development: A Study of High Flyers.* Oxford: Blackwell.

Yeatman, A. 1994. *Postmodern Revisionings of the Political.* London: Routledge.

Zeldin, T. 1995. *An Intimate History of Humanity.* London: Minerva.

CHAPTER TWO

# Changing Gender Scripts and Moral Dilemmas for Women and Men in Education, 1940–1970

Cecilia Reynolds

*Canada*

## INTRODUCTION

The discussion in this chapter grows out of reflection on research and writing on gender and leadership which I have undertaken in a variety of studies over the past several years. While focused on the Canadian educational context, much of that work has implications beyond that setting and speaks to the impact of changes over time in the ways that men and women have come to understand and take up dominant "scripts" in school cultures. My first question is: How does the history of gender relations in schools inform our views about school leadership?

Lortie (1975) has commented that, "There is nothing obvious about the ways that people are routed into various kinds of work in modern society," and he argues that people's seemingly personal decisions actually "interact with social constraints to produce the aggregate of individual decisions which result in movement into a given occupation" (25). Hargreaves (1994) has pointed out that:

> Most of the problems that the teacher encounters . . . have faced similarly placed colleagues in the past. Over the years these colleagues develop ways of doing things, along with whole networks of associated educational beliefs and values. . . . Culture carries the community's historically generated and collectively shared solutions. . . . Cultures of teaching help give meaning, support, and identity to teachers and their work. (217)

What are the social constraints that women and men encounter as they become school leaders? How have these changed over time? How have they affected people's decisions about leadership? How have past school leaders shaped change while at the same time responding to it? To examine these questions, this chapter considers both the broad context and the decision-making processes of a small sample of men and women in the postwar generation, the1940s and 1950s, and the employment equity generation, the 1960s and 1970s.

What is called into question in this chapter are ways that we might conceptualize "change" and how we might consider what changes in the larger context mean to men and women who work in educational systems. I argue that when we focus on the micropolitics of gender and school leadership, it is crucial to consider the "macropolitics" of gender in given historical periods. The discussion in this chapter is predicated on the view that sex/gender is intricately related to ideas about womanhood and manhood, ideas that "develop, change, and are combined, amended and contested" (Bederman 1995, 7) in different ways, in different times, and in different places.

## HISTORICAL AND LONGITUDINAL RESEARCH

Much of what we know about gender and school leadership comes from empirical studies that use a social science "snapshot" approach; that is, data are collected at a particular time and place (Glesne and Peshkin 1992, 154). Historical approaches using archival materials and life history interviews are less common, as are attempts to develop longitudinal data bases where individuals or groups are followed over an extended period of time (Neuman 1997, 381).

All research methods have their own set of limitations and can provide us with only a partial analysis of the phenomenon under study. In order to obtain longitudinal data, researchers often must limit themselves to a small group of informants, and they must work with whatever materials are available. Such researchers must be patient sleuths who look for clues and patterns across data sets. In this form of research, as in most qualitative research, generalization is not the aim. The investigator wishes instead to deepen insights by providing rich descriptions of complex issues. As is the case in this chapter, the main aim of this sort of research is to develop and refine frameworks, or useful "ways of seeing," which inform and lead to further questions.

This chapter draws on a life history interview study. The data from that study are examined here with a focus on changing gender relations in Canadian schools. Also under scrutiny are the meaning-making practices and self-described moral dilemmas of a small group of men and women principals over a thirty-year span from 1940 to 1970. The quest is to consider how to "theorize gender in a way that reflects the 'lived' reality of this experience" (Eisenstein 1993, 8) without overemphasizing choice as idiosyncratic and disassociating it from contextual factors. I am curious about how to make sense of what men and women leaders have experienced in order to examine the relative "power of women as a political force" and their "political leverage" (ibid.) in particular school contexts. In other words, how does the past inform the present?

## SELF AND MORALITY AS REVEALED IN LIFE HISTORIES— METHODS AND FRAMEWORKS

In 1987, I conducted life history interviews with twenty-four men and women who taught and then became principals of elementary or secondary schools in the Toronto Board of Education. Six men and six women were from the 1940s' and 1950s' generation. An additional six men and six women were from the next generation, the 1960s and 1970s. In this large study, lengthy interviews were supplemented with personal archival documents. The life histories were examined against a backdrop of historical literature about teaching in the province of Ontario (Prentice 1977; Gaskell, McLaren, and Novogrodsky 1989; Gidney and Millar 1990; Reynolds and Young 1995; Reynolds 1998).

The data set from this life history study have been examined here to identify and examine self-described moral dilemmas that these men and women experienced when they decided to become principals. What conceptions of self and morality are evident in the data? To address this question, a theoretical lens about morality is needed.

Greenfield (1995) has argued that schools should be construed as moral enterprises. Not only do those who work in school settings feel a moral obligation to the students under their care, they make a number of work-related decisions based primarily on their personal beliefs about what to do in a given situation. Lyons (1988) has placed morality itself under scrutiny with regard to gender, and she has argued that there are at least two perspectives. First, morality may be seen as a way of knowing what one ought to do, or what is right. This view is the one that she feels currently holds sway in both psychological research and in the popular imagination. It relies on the image of "a person in a discrete moment of individual choice" (22). A second view of morality, however, considers it as a sensitivity or type of consciousness, which "incorporates an injunction not to hurt other people" (21). This view of morality relies on the image of individuals who see themselves as connected and attending to others.

Studies incorporating these two perspectives on morality, such as those described in *Mapping the Moral Domain* (Gilligan, Ward, and Taylor 1988), suggest that most males self-define as "separate or objective" and employ a view of morality as something enacted in a "discrete moment of rational choosing" (Lyons 1988, 21), whereas most females self-define as "predominately connected" and see morality as something rooted in time but "not bounded by the single moment" (22). Is this gender pattern with regard to morality born out in the life history data of the men and women principals I studied? Does the pattern hold across changing contexts for different generations? Examination of the data for the postwar generation illustrates some commonalities within gender groups and some differences between them with regard to decisions to take on the principalship.

## THE POSTWAR GENERATION:
## DUTIFUL DAUGHTERS AND REAL MEN

What were the dominant gender scripts available in Canadian society following the Second World War? Following a general description of historical context, this section of the chapter provides excerpts from the life history interviews as evidence of how some men and women made decisions about school leadership roles in the 1940s and 1950s. I argue, based on these data, that for women in these decades, the dominant script appears to have been that of the "dutiful daughter" who stayed close to home, made a contribution of service to the community, and often sacrificed her own wishes to satisfy the needs of the school organization.

Data from men in the 1940s and 1950s suggested that teaching was a role that did not mesh easily with the dominant script for "real men" in the society. The principalship, however, offered a masculine script within schools where most men could feel comfortable and accepted. Men in this era admitted that being a male had been an advantage in terms of attaining a principalship.

### THE GENERAL CONTEXT

Politics and the economy in Canada in the 1940s and 1950s, as in so many parts of the world, were dominated by the events of the Second World War. During that war, gender roles had come under scrutiny in contradictory ways (Mandell 1995, 332). On the one hand, women had participated during the war effort in some very nontraditional ways. On the other hand, once the war was over, there was a government-sponsored, "back to the home" push (Light and Pierson 1989) that urged women to leave paid employment and enjoy being full-time homemakers and mothers.

Important critics of the location of women in the Canadian society in this era were feminist trade unionist Madeline Parent, who organized textile workers in Quebec, and historian Hilda Neatby, who wrote the critique of Canadian education titled *So Little for the Mind*. In 1951, another feminist, Nellie McClung, died after playing a pivotal role in fostering debates about women's role in Canadian society. McClung had been a schoolteacher, author, and controversial member of the Alberta legislature. She was a major player in the famous "persons" case in the 1920s, whereby women in Canada became eligible to hold a seat in the Canadian Senate. She urged women to, "Never retract, never explain, never apologize—get things done and let them howl" (quoted in Mandell 1995, 334).

## The Context in the Toronto Board of Education

The 1941 Canada census showed that 75 percent of all teachers were women (although this was a drop from a previous high in 1921, when 82 percent had been women) (Reynolds 1987b). In the Toronto Board, while most teachers were women, most school principals were men. Over 95 percent of all elementary schools in the Toronto Board were headed by male principals, and only 2 out of 18 secondary schools in that era had a female principal (Reynolds 1990).

What was the configuration of gender relations within the Toronto Board during the 1940s and 1950s? Archival materials provide some clues. For example, records show that a marriage ban, developed in 1925 (requiring that all women resign their teaching post immediately upon marriage), came under fire in the postwar period and was rescinded in 1947 (Reynolds 1987a). The rhetoric in the debate over this policy change was full of talk about gender equality but, as I have argued elsewhere (Reynolds 1990), this change can also be interpreted as a pragmatic organizational response to a teacher shortage tied to the rising birthrate. Documents also indicate that the practice of automatically paying a salary "bonus" to all male teachers was hotly contested and eventually discontinued in this time period.

These archival documents suggest that long-standing and clear distinctions between the roles or scripts available to men and women teachers in the board came under pressure during the postwar period. As political, economic, and social contexts changed in the 1940s and 1950s, a rhetoric of equality began to carry more weight within the wider culture and the culture of the board. While discussions of demographic patterns and changes in policies and practices help us recognize changing contexts, if we wish to understand how individual men and women made sense of these contexts, we need to look at personal accounts such as those obtained through life history interviews.

## SELF AND MORALITY AS REVEALED
## IN LIFE HISTORY ACCOUNTS

### Becoming a Principal—The Men

The six men studied from the postwar generation of the 1940s and 1950s admitted that classroom life had been a mixture of pleasure and pain. They spent an average of eighteen years in the classroom before becoming principals. They felt that, because they were men, they had been given some tough assignments in rural schools. Some also stated that expectations around their behavior as teachers had posed moral dilemmas. Several of these themes are evident in the following excerpts from the men's descriptions of their life as classroom teachers:

> I was hired sight unseen in Northern Peterborough . . . I taught all the grades from one to eight. It was a standard rural school in the bush. (Reynolds 1987b, 51)

> One thing they emphasized was no smoking. . . . Most schools at that time did not want smokers. You had to be a moral old maid, really. That was it. (Reynolds 1987b, 57)

> Working in the country was a shock. . . . You did the best you could. I didn't drink or smoke . . . I saved for a car to get the hell out of that place. (Reynolds 1987b, 52)

> I ran a boxing club. We put on dances and raised money . . . we played hockey. . . . The dividends were tremendous in terms of personal satisfaction. (Reynolds 1987b, 62)

Each of the men studied in this generation admitted that he experienced privileges within the school system simply because he was a man. The following quotes indicate that salary was one of the most overt ways that this was evident:

> It was the time when women weren't getting as much money as men. The rub came when a few women . . . who were helping me learn to teach . . . were getting $700 and I was getting $1600. . . . They rose above it and so did I, but thank God they did. (Reynolds 1987b, 62)

> Men were in short supply. So, I'm not so vain to think it was just my great talents. I happened to teach Math. I was a man. I had experience. Where could you find a man with experience to teach Math? (Reynolds 1987b, 62)

> Being the only man there was a great thing in my favor. . . . If they were all men teachers, wouldn't the woman teacher be the delight of the kids? (Reynolds 1987b, 62)

While admitting to some dilemmas concerning their position of privilege in the system compared to their female peers, men studied in this generation were quite comfortable with being asked to move from the classroom to the principal's office. There was little, if any, conflict between what they saw as being good for self and for others in the school system. Using the framework from Lyons (1988) on morality, it appears that the men studied in this generation were operating within a morality of justice that affected their decision to become a principal. The next logical step in their career path as autonomous individuals, due to obligations to their family was to move forward, if possible, in order to provide improved economic benefits and a more secure future. As indicated in the quotes that follow, the men studied felt that the agreement to take on the principalship was a reward for past success, a type of reciprocity.

Many of the men stated that they had actively sought promotion and had expected to receive it. They also indicated that they felt they knew how to play the leadership game.

> I always felt that teaching elementary was hardly a job for a man. I was vaguely dissatisfied. In those days I wasn't proud of it . . . I thought the principalship would be an easy job. (Reynolds 1987b, 62)

> I wasn't career planning at first . . . I got restless . . . my wife stayed home and the mortgage was a problem . . . there was a vague career path developing now . . . after three years in secondary teaching I became a vice-principal. I was hustling for that. (Reynolds 1987b, 82)

> I knew the system. I knew the people. As we would say in the army, I knew the whole drill . . . I had the feeling that I was slated for further promotion. . . . You never turn down an opportunity . . . I wasn't causing any trouble. (Reynolds 1987b, 82)

Clearly, gender played an important part in the decisions and experiences of men studied in this generation, as they moved out of the classroom and into the principalship. Yet the descriptions offered indicate that they saw their movement as primarily an individual response to opportunity. They saw choosing to become a principal as a discrete action at a given point in time, and they did not stress the need to stay connected to the classroom or to the students. Each of the men studied was married with children. Their decisions around the principalship encompassed their responsibilities to that family, as well as to the school organization.

## Becoming a Principal—The Women

The six women studied from the generation of the 1940s and 1950s averaged twenty-one years in classrooms before becoming school principals (five to ten years longer than the males in the study from the same era). While the men reported eagerly accepting the chance to become a principal, the women talked about resisting the move out of the classroom. The following series of quotes indicates the women's love of their classroom roles and their hesitancy about moving into the principalship:

> It was a cozy staff. There was a women teachers' lunchroom and a men teachers' lunchroom. You could smoke in the furnace room . . . I was the first woman to be allowed to teach Accounting. (Reynolds 1987b, 67)

> I enjoyed that school . . . I didn't see why I should go to that other school . . . I was ready to resign . . . I phoned my parents and told them I was coming home. Anyway, the vice-principal talked me out of it. . . . Part of it was that it would be administration . . . I'd be away from the youngsters . . . I didn't know if I wanted any more headaches. I used to think

anyone who was a principal of a school was nuts. Principals were people who ruled the roost. I wasn't that kind of person . . . I said: "Well, if you think I am the right person, I'll try it." (Reynolds 1987b, 80)

I was happy where I was and I just didn't want to leave. . . . It was just a foreign land to me . . . I began to get the message that I wasn't going to have much choice . . . I finally said to him: "I'll try it for two years but I want a guarantee that if I don't like it, I will go back where I was." (Reynolds 1987b, 81)

Each of the women studied in this generation remembered that she had been encouraged by superiors to take on a "troubled" school for the good of the children and the school board. One woman described it this way:

Women have been given most of the "clean-up" jobs. Men could do those jobs but more often than not, they have been allotted to females. (Reynolds 1987b, 99)

Another woman in the study agreed that women had been given most of the difficult postings in the board. She explained it this way:

I think the women I know and work with seem to be people who can deal with awkward situations. So, maybe they have been given them to deal with because of that. We may have bought our own fate. (Reynolds 1987b, 99)

The women agreed that being a "lady principal" had been difficult at a personal level. Part of that had to do with their relations with the male principals in the board, as illustrated by this comment:

As principals we had arrived. Now I want to say that the acceptance was not without shock on the part of some of the male principals. . . . One man said to me: "I just never thought of having a woman as a principal. Men have a family to support and so forth and women shouldn't be getting the salary." It wasn't a nasty non-acceptance. I mean they tried to be nice to me. But I remember that I went to a conference and sat down in the middle row and nobody sat beside me. (Reynolds 1987b, 98)

Data from the women in the 1940s and 1950s suggest that becoming a principal posed a moral dilemma for them concerning duty to themselves and to others in the school community. Should they place their own comfort level ahead of the needs of the children and the school system as a whole? Who should come first, self or others? Should they abandon their relationships with peers, mainly women, and adopt a role that entailed obligations, duties, and commitments that were valued within the larger system but that might change the level of care they had come to accept in their teaching role? Should they operate within a morality of justice, as described by Lyons (1988), or continue within a morality of response and care, which had initially led them into the teaching profession?

The women studied moved into the principalship with ambivalence. Theirs was a journey across a dangerous border into "male territory," where they were tolerated but not necessarily welcome. This woman's account of her experience, as she attended a course designed to prepare people for their role as principal, makes a point about male territory:

> There were only three women on the principal's course and that was the first year that I began to understand how blacks feel, because there were a lot of people who were nice to me but there were men who you would catch looking at you as if they were asking "What are you doing here?" I was trespassing in an area where I had no right to be trespassing. (Reynolds 1987b, 81)

Access had been granted to women and girls in the postwar era to many scripts within school culture, which had previously been seen as only appropriate for males. Social and organizational structures in school systems frequently maintained a "chilly climate" for females who took up these scripts. Schools borrowed from the discourse of human resource management, prevalent in business and industry in the 1940s and 1950s, to support claims that it was wise to use the skills of women and girls. Claims about gender difference, however, were muted by a rhetoric of equality that posited that equality meant sameness. Girls and women were expected to be grateful for their new privileges and to obey the rules in a quiet, "ladylike" fashion.

One of the costs of taking up the lady principal script in this era revolved around marital status and mothering. None of the women I studied in this generation had children. Some had never married; those who had talked about deciding to forego having children. The women principals explained that their decision regarding childbearing was related to a desire to fulfill their responsibilities as a school leader, a role they believed required obvious commitment to their paid work.

## THE EMPLOYMENT EQUITY GENERATION: SUPERWOMEN AND GOOD GUYS

How did scripts available to women and men in Canadian society change in the 1960s and 1970s? Despite some identifiable changes in historical context, excerpts from life history interviews with women principals of the 1960s and 1970s suggest that some women continued to enact the dutiful daughter script and take on a lady principal role similar to that from the past. Many of these women accepted support from powerful male "fathers" within the system. Other women, however, enacted a new "Superwoman" script, a script also described in greater detail by Blackmore in the next chapter. This script placed women between what Acker (1999) has called two "greedy" institutions—the school and the family. The Superwoman script of this era challenged women to juggle work and home responsibilities, without dropping any of the balls. Combining the Superwoman script with a "woman principal" script allowed some women to openly challenge hiring and promotion procedures. Some went as far as asserting new "womanly" ways of leading, ways that threatened to change the leadership game in schools.

Men studied in the 1960s and 1970s continued to admit that being a male privileged them in many ways within school systems. For most men in these decades, movement from the teacher role to the principalship contin- ued to be a route that made sense. It offered them recognition, monetary reward, and an affirmation of their masculinity. In this era, however, the data suggest that a new "good guy" script was being taken up by some men who wanted to overtly display caring and nurturing behaviors and attitudes. The men who combined the principal and good guy scripts talked about "people skills" and the ways that they supported women, and they wanted to work for equity in schools.

## THE GENERAL CONTEXT

The 1960s and 1970s in Canada were decades when human rights activists marched and society questioned various forms of authority. For much of this period, the Canadian economy was strong. Children of the baby boom era filled the schools. It was also a time when significant legislation, such as the Canadian Human Rights Act (1977), was passed, which protected women from discrimination and promised them equal pay for work of equal value. While "affirmative action" policies were being developed in the United States at this time, in Canada, similar initiatives took up the phrase "employment equity" (Abella 1991).

The 1962 census showed that women made up 30 percent of the paid labor force in Canada. By 1976, the census showed that for every 100 marriages in Canada, there were twenty-eight divorces, and while the average income for a female-headed household was $9,001, a male-headed household averaged $21,551 (Mandell 1995, 337–43). Feminist leaders of this era included Laura Sabia, a politician instrumental in establishing the National Action Committee on the Status of Women (NAC), and Doris Anderson, the controversial editor of the popular women's journal *Chatelaine* (1958–1977). Another feminist was Pauline Jewitt, an educator and a politician, who became the first woman pres- ident of a major coed Canadian university when she took up the post at Simon Fraser University (1974–1978) (Mandell 1995, 340).

## THE CONTEXT IN THE TORONTO BOARD OF EDUCATION

By 1961, 71 percent of all elementary and secondary teachers in Canada were women, but by 1971, that number had slipped to 66 percent. There were significant shifts in the teacher population by marital status, and well over half of all male and female teachers across the country were married (Reynolds 1983). In the Toronto Board, the number of elementary schools doubled between 1960 and 1970, and the number of secondary schools grew from eighteen to twenty-six, but at both levels approximately 90 percent of the principals were men (Reynolds 1990). World events, such as the space age, had placed a new emphasis on schooling. The percentage of students obtaining a high school diploma gradually increased. Access to colleges and universities for males and females from all class, race, and ethnic groups was a topic of heated debate. Increasing percentages of parents in Toronto became politically active and challenged teachers and school leaders on a number of school issues (Dehli 1996). Within the board, archival documents reveal that a number of feminist teachers, as well as administrators and members of the board's elected trustees, actively pursued an agenda of gender equity for both students and teachers. This was manifested in new policies with regard to hiring procedures and in special programs and resources aimed at female students (Gaskell et al. 1989). As a result, gender relations were once again under scrutiny, but this time a new discourse of diversity (see Blackmore's discussion in the next chapter) framed much of the gender equity debate within the Toronto Board.

## SELF AND MORALITY AS REVEALED
## IN LIFE HISTORY ACCOUNTS

### BECOMING A PRINCIPAL—THE MEN

The amount of time men in this generation spent in the classroom before they became principals was shorter than that of men in the previous generation. It was also somewhat shorter than that reported for women in the study in this generation. The six men studied averaged eleven years in the classroom. The shortest time reported was six years, and the longest was thirteen years.

Men studied in the 1960s and 1970s, like those in the 1940s and 1950s, made many negative comments about the limitations that conditions in schools had placed on them as teachers. For example, one man remarked:

> I had a really tough time . . . I got the dregs of the world. Young teachers
> often get those. It was difficult. I lost a lot of sleep. I had stomach problems.
> I solved it in the second year, but the first was bad. (Reynolds 1987b, 59)

In the quotes that follow, the comments of men of this generation, about how and why they chose to become principals, suggest a shared view of autonomous and separate individuals who needed to make a good choice among the available alternatives, rather than a connected self concerned with maintaining relationships. There is evidence in the following statements of beliefs about reciprocity, an element that Lyons (1988) claims is part of a morality of justice:

> One tends to get sort of ambitious, although I never was one to advance over someone else's dead body. . . . Toronto was expanding. There were many more opportunities for advancement than there had been in the previous twenty years. (Reynolds 1987b, 85)

> I loved my school, but I knew the incumbent retired in a couple of years and I changed my mind. I had talked it over with my wife . . . I felt I was more than ready. (Reynolds 1987b, 85)

> To move up meant two things; recognition for what you have done and more money. (Reynolds 1987b, 85)

## BECOMING A PRINCIPAL—THE WOMEN

Each of the six women studied in the second generation described a "turning point" that encouraged her to consider moving into the principalship. Unlike women in the first generation, this group tended to see the move into the principalship as a discrete moment of choice and thus they were more like men in the two generations studied. The women studied from the 1960s and 1970s explained that they decided to become principals because they wanted to do more than just help children. Comments by these two women illustrate this sentiment:

> I had decided that I was going to work for the rest of my life, and I did not want to . . . spend the next thirty-five years, which literally it would be, in the English classroom. I saw that as making me very narrow and limited as an educator. (Reynolds 1987b, 19)

> I had done something I loved for nine years, but I wanted to do more than help children. (Reynolds 1987b, 83)

The women in this generation tended to spend less time than women in the previous generation as classroom teachers before becoming principals. They averaged thirteen years in the classroom. While, overall, women in this generation spoke positively about their time in classrooms, they, like the men in the two generations discussed, noted negative aspects about school life. The following quotes spell out some of their insights:

> The school was like a huge grey prison, all grey stone. . . . There were 3,000 students in that school. It was like a small town . . . I liked the kids, and I liked the staff. . . . It felt like a good place to be. (Reynolds 1987b, 60)

I resolved that if I were going to stay in teaching, I would upgrade my own qualifications and I would work for equal pay for equal kinds of work and also be involved with trying to get people to do equal things in an extra-curricular way. . . . Yard duties always had to have a man. . . . There was lots to be done, and people were prepared to let a certain group of us do the work. (Reynolds 1987b, 64)

Women in both generations stressed the emotional work they did as teachers in the classroom, but women in this later generation also talked about emotional work they did with their male peers and their male superiors in trying to ensure that they and other women were recognized within the system. The following quotes indicate that, in this era, there was more than one route open for women who wished to become principals:

The principal was the one who persuaded me . . . I knew that I wanted to leave the confines of my classroom and be responsible for a greater number of kids. I didn't feel reluctant, but I was concerned about having to leave my good friends at that school. (Reynolds 1987b, 84)

That man was a great influence in my career. He was a man I highly respected. . . . People always sought me out all through my career. (Reynolds 1987b, 83)

I simply identified myself, and they supported me and said, "Yeah, you'd be great. Go for it." The first year they came and observed me, I didn't get the nod, so I said, "Well, I'm going to do it again." (Reynolds 1987b, 84)

I found out that the superintendent had not even been prepared to consider my application because I had four children and he thought I couldn't spare the time. But a man I had worked with . . . went down and went to bat for me. (Reynolds 1987b, 84)

These data suggest diversity for this generation of women with regard to their sense of self as autonomous and/or connected. Women in the study agreed that feminist and employment equity debates within school systems and the general society had resulted in an overall shift in attitudes toward women as leaders. As "newcomers" to leadership levels in this school board, the women from this generation reported that they felt like immigrants to a new land. They were not exactly welcomed by those in power, but they were tolerated due to a somewhat protected location. Overt actions against them were not "politically correct." In a time when many people worried about "reverse discrimination," this woman reported, however, that being a woman principal often carried a price that not all women wanted to pay:

When you went to meetings at the principal or vice-principal level, there were few of us, and there were times when I purposely said that I didn't want to be identified with the other women . . . I wasn't aware of how I was coping and giving in to things . . . accepting those racist and sexist jokes . . . I used to laugh, because I wanted to be one of the boys. I don't laugh anymore. (Reynolds 1987b, 101)

To varying degrees, the six women studied from this generation exhibited a sense of themselves, not just as individuals but as members of the category "women." Some of those studied identified themselves as feminists, but even those who shied away from that label revealed in their accounts ways that they were aware of the language and the opportunities that feminism presented in this era. The comments from those in this generation suggest that, unlike the previous generation of lady principals, these women wanted to lay open for scrutiny the process of becoming a principal. They wanted a level playing field and a fair game.

The school principalship, while advertised by the organization in the 1960s and 1970s as a place where diversity could flourish, was, by the accounts in the life history study, still a very traditional environment that offered limited, highly gendered scripts to both men and women. It is hard to argue that things had improved overall for principals studied across these two generations, but it is clear that their experiences differed across the generations and across gender groups in the shifting contexts.

## CONCLUSIONS

What is revealed by a consideration of the context of the 1940s and 1950s and the dilemmas recounted by men and women who became principals during that time frame? We can see that while the society was allowing some regendering of roles such as the principalship, there were strong political and economic forces mitigating against an increase in women's overall participation alongside men in the same roles and at the same rates of pay. While a few women made dramatic individual moves, most took up traditional roles. The official government position was one of laissez-faire, and organizations such as schools were able to maintain rules of operation suited to those groups that had traditionally held power within them.

In school systems, such as the Toronto Board of Education, this meant that very few women were likely to be invited to take on the principal's role. Those who were invited were chosen because of particular individual skills, and areas of need within the board. It was a wise deployment of human resources. The women selected were unlikely to be seen as radicals or to be self-declared feminists and were more likely to be seen as good, organizational citizens who would obey the rules. Thus, according to Blackmore's discussion in chapter 3 of this book, these women were not seen "as trouble," but their reports show that at least some of them found themselves "in trouble" as they struggled to deal with their circumstances. In response, rather than working against the grain, those in this study decided to appear to be playing the game while often unobtrusively adapting that game at the local level. These women expected a lot of themselves in terms of making personal sacrifices for the good of the school.

In this era, the structures of the school organization positioned the male principal as the norm, and thus women principals were positioned as "other." The data suggest that these women found themselves in a precarious personal location as they struggled to be true to themselves and to their organizational role. They talked about how difficult it had been to exercise power since, when they behaved like women, they felt they were not taken seriously. Yet they could not present themselves as being exactly like men either. They were caught in a "gender bind" that diminished their personal and organizational power.

The six women studied from the postwar generation, however, found a variety of ways to act, despite their limited social and political location. They talked about deciding to focus their leadership energies. Each, in her own way, concentrated her energies on the school, on teachers, on parents, and/or on students. The women sometimes used their positions as lady principals to undertake things that were contrary to existing rules. Several commented that it was more effective to ask forgiveness than to ask for permission. Repeatedly, they described having done what they thought was best for their school, but they remembered that they had been careful not to appear to be upsetting larger power structures. Their efforts toward change were largely at the micro level. While outwardly appearing to conform, they carried out small acts of resistance and sometimes even rebellion, acts that could be called "innocent subversion" because of an outward appearance of not knowing the rules but an admitted attempt to improve the overall situation. As such, they were extremely visible in the organization. An oddity, yet within that subject position (Davies 1993) or gender script, they were able to carry out some equity reforms at the local level.

There were limits, however, to what these principals could accomplish. Although they reported trying to help girls and other women whenever they could, the principals also described feeling unable to do much in that regard. Cast as pioneers within the larger school culture, these women could cut the path but could do little to ensure that it would remain open for others. The emphasis of their era was on the individual and, while these pioneers could give other individual women a push ahead, they could do little to alter large-scale policies and practices within the board. Women in this generation did not talk about taking up the task of transforming the school system, a job taken on by some of the women in the next generation of the 1960s and 1970s.

In the employment equity generation of the 1960s and 1970s, the women studied reported somewhat different dilemmas about becoming a school principal than those expressed by women from the previous generation.

These women felt it was personally important for them to come forward to lead at the school level. They saw the principalship as a desirable position which, if attained, was a form of organizational recognition of their abilities and their commitment to the school and to the profession. These women applied for the principalship rather than being selected. A common dilemma for them concerned how to act when procedures were less than equitable. They worried about being branded as a troublemaker if they complained, but they also did not want to let themselves be the victims of unfair practices, or to have those practices perpetuated in ways that would hurt other women. Having been successful in gaining a principalship, they admitted worrying about whether it was merit based, on individual ability, or whether the board's desire to be seen promoting more women was behind their success. None of those interviewed wanted to think that they had been tokens. They wanted to fix up the flaws they noted in current procedures within the organization, procedures that hindered them and other women, as well as some of the men, they worked with.

The women studied commented that they did not want to have to portray themselves as twice as qualified as male competitors when they applied for promotions. Nor did they want to have to work twice as hard as male peers once they became principals (Dempsey and Reynolds 1989). While these women felt that they had benefited from male and female mentors, they saw problems with establishing an "old girl's network" that was filled with the same problems as the "old boy's network," which they knew was operating in the organization. These women principals claimed power in ways that were similar to those being undertaken by female students and students of color in colleges and universities in Canada and elsewhere during this time period. These women spoke a discourse of diversity (see Blackmore in the next chapter for a further discussion of the limits of this discourse). They drew upon the language of human relations familiar in the business world at the time. It was good management practice to present the organization as one that treated its members fairly and allowed those with talent to rise to the top. These women did not see a move to the principalship as a sacrifice but rather as a reward.

Like the generation before them, however, these women worried about being feminine, and about being a good leader at the same time. They had a dilemma over how to balance their home and work responsibilities. Many had children and husbands; some did not. Even those who lived alone worried about having to set priorities between private and public worlds. The women with crowded households discussed having to educate their families about shared duties and responsibilities. Just as in their paid work, these women sought out procedures or ways of handling their unpaid work that were fair and equitable. All of the women interviewed from this era struggled with wanting it all and having to be "Superwoman." Several reported marital breakdowns related to their leadership aspirations. Unlike the preceding generation, many talked about hiring domestic help, especially for child care. These women described dilemmas that involved when to take time off from work to deal with sick family members and when to prioritize the needs of the school. They wanted to be professionals, but they also wanted to fulfill their roles as women in their private settings.

Several women studied in this generation commented about wanting to free themselves from imperatives to always be warm and friendly, caring and nurturing. They saw this as an unfair gender stereotype that frequently diminished their contributions in the organization and hindered their ability to portray themselves as strong leaders who could handle confrontation and conflict. Dilemmas formed as these women tried to deal with tough human relations issues in their schools, and policy issues, in the larger system, when staff and parents expected them to be focused only on the individual needs of each child. One woman described how difficult it had been to fulfill the expectations others held for a woman in the principal's role:

> I thought I was going to be God's gift to them. They didn't view it that way, and they certainly didn't view a woman that way. The male parents and the women teachers in that school did not approve of this person, so I had a hard time . . . I learned not to keep all my troubles to myself. It was a very small staff, and when I told them about the petition the parents had mounted against me, they all rallied around. I was glad I had stuck to my guns. (Reynolds 1987b, 100)

While women in the previous generation had been limited by being positioned as "other," it appears that all of the women studied in this generation were limited by being positioned as "mother," whether or not they had any biological offspring. They ran into trouble when their individual actions, which they saw as unrelated to gender, were viewed as gender related by others.

How did women in the employment equity generation focus their leadership energies? Some of these women principals worked overtly to foster political agendas aimed at transforming the system, such as striving for employment equity policies within the board. Others focused on their own individual career route. These women principals talked about weighing the personal and political costs of their actions as women and individuals, both within the organization and outside of it. Only slightly less visible and vulnerable than the women of the previous generation, these women principals still had to think seriously about to what extent they could question the rules of the leadership game and how much they could try to change those rules and still be allowed to play.

What is revealed by looking across these two generations? We can see that women have not always found themselves in the same power position in different eras, even when they have taken on similar roles. A variety of factors in the larger society, and within the school board, as an organization, worked to offer different scripts to men and women over time as they took on the role of principal. Thus it should not be assumed that women in that role, at different times and in different places, had the same political leverage, since this could vary according to a wide array of factors, as we have seen in the material presented in this chapter. Variations in the power of women as a political force in the society and the institution are only part of the picture. There also was evidence in the data of variations in the principalship itself over time and in the ways in which men and women conceived of self and morality.

Looking across these generations, we can see how different gendered scripts for principals came to dominate in changing historical contexts. We also can see that individual men and women, while aware of the dominant scripts, took up or read from a range of scripts, or what Davies (1993) calls subject positions, in creative ways. Like actors in a play, or dancers (Hall 1997), they pulled from a repertoire of skills and personal attributes to interpret the scripts. Their audiences, by their accounts, however, frequently saw their portrayal, or dance, only in relation to what was deemed acceptable for men and women in the time period. Organizational structures and available discourses were important in terms of how men and women viewed school leadership and structures and how discourses affected the ways in which they decided to pick up, alter, or discard available leadership scripts.

While the discussion in this chapter clearly illustrates that dominant scripts changed for men and women in school leadership over this thirty-year span, it is less clear whether these changes represented improvements in gender relations or in the overall political leverage of women in school organizations. It often is tempting to ask whether things are getting better for women leaders in education. Perhaps this question is too simple, given the complexities discussed in this chapter. Looking, as we have here, at the history of gender relations in schools and the patterns discernible in the meaning-making practices of men and women principals in different generations suggests a view of leadership as a multifaceted puzzle that shifts even as we try to enact it or study it.

## REFERENCES

Abella, R. 1991. "Equality and Human Rights in Canada: Coping with the New Isms." *University Affairs* (June/July): 21–22.

Acker, S. 1999. *The Realities of Teachers' Work: Never a Dull Moment.* New York: Cassell.

Bederman, G. 1995. *Manliness and Civilization: A Cultural History of Gender and Race in the United States, 1880–1917.* Chicago: University of Chicago Press.

Davies, B. 1993. *Shards of Glass: Children Reading and Writing beyond Gendered Identities.* Cresskill, N.J.: Hampton Press.

Delhi, K. 1996. "Between Market and State? Engendering Education in the 1990s." *Discourses: Studies in the Cultural Politics of Education* 17:3:363–76.

Dempsey, S., and C. Reynolds. 1989. "A Comparison of How Men and Women Supervisory Officers Spend Their Time." *Journal of Educational Administration and Foundations* 7:1:58–71.

Eisenstein, H. 1993. "A Telling Tale from the Field." Pp. 1–8 in *Gender Matters in Educational Administration and Policy*, ed. J. Blackmore et al. Washington: Falmer Press.

Gaskell, J., A. McLaren, and M. Novogrodsky. 1989. *Claiming an Education: Feminism and Canadian Schools.* Toronto: Our Schools/Ourselves Education Foundation.

Gidney, R., and W. Millar. 1990. *Inventing Secondary Education.* Montreal: McGill-Queen's University Press.

Gilligan, C., J. Ward, and J. Taylor. 1988. *Mapping the Moral Domain: A Contribution of Women's Thinking to Psychological Theory and Education.* Cambridge: Harvard University Press.

Glesne, C., and A. Peshkin. 1992. *Becoming Qualitative Researchers: An Introduction.* White Plains, N.Y. : Longman.

Greenfield, W. D., Jr. 1995. "Toward a Theory of School Administration: The Centrality of Leadership." *Education Administration Quarterly* 3:91:61–81.

Hall, V. 1997. *Dancing on the Ceiling: A Study of Women Managers in Education.* London: Paul Chapman.

Hargreaves, A. 1994. *Changing Teachers, Changing Times: Teachers' Work and Culture in the Postmodern Age.* Toronto: OISE Press.

Light, B., and R. Pierson, eds. 1989. *No Easy Road.* Toronto: New Hogtown Press.

Lortie, D. C. 1975. *Schoolteacher: A Sociological Study.* Chicago: University of Chicago Press.

Lyons, N. 1988. "Two Perspectives: On Self, Relationships, and Morality." Pp. 21–48 in *Mapping the Moral Domain: A Contribution of Women's Thinking to Psychological Theory and Education*, C. Gilligan et al. Cambridge: Harvard University Press.

Mandell, N., ed. 1995. *Feminist Issues: Race, Class, and Sexuality.* Scarborough: Prentice Hall Canada Inc.

Neuman, W. L. 1997. *Social Research Methods: Qualitative and Quantitative Approaches*, 3d ed. Needham Heights, Mass.: Allyn & Bacon.

Prentice, A. 1977. "The Feminization of Teaching." Pp. 49–65 in *The Neglected Majority*, ed. S. Trofimenkoff and A. Prentice. Toronto: McClelland & Stewart.

Reynolds, C. 1983. "Ontario Schoolteachers, 1911–1971: A Portrait of Demographic Change." Unpublished master's thesis, University of Toronto.

Reynolds, C. 1987a. "Limited Liberation: A Policy on Married Women Teachers." Pp. 215–22 in *Women Educators: Employees of Schools in Western Countries*, ed. Patricia Schmuck. Albany: State University of New York Press.

Reynolds, C. 1987b. "Naming the Experience: Women, Men, and Their Changing Worklives As Teachers and Principals." Unpublished doctoral dissertation, University of Toronto.

Reynolds, C. 1990. "Hegemony and Hierarchy: Becoming a Teacher in Toronto, 1930–1980." *Historical Studies in Education* 2:1:95–119.

Reynolds, C. 1998. "Why Does This Feel Like the Margins, I Thought I Was at the Center?" Paper presented at the Canadian Association for the Study of Women in Education Summer Institute, "Centering on the Margins: The Evaded Curriculum," Ottawa.

Reynolds, C., and B. Young, eds. 1995. *Women and Leadership in Canadian Education.* Calgary: Temeron Books.

# CHAPTER THREE

# TROUBLING WOMEN:
# THE UPSIDES AND DOWNSIDES OF LEADERSHIP
# AND THE NEW MANAGERIALISM

Jill Blackmore

*Australia*

## THE "NEW" MANAGERIALISM

In this chapter, I examine the "new managerialism," a phenomenon born out of the material and cultural conditions of globalization. I argue that the new managerialism supports a politics of diversity that is ultimately assimilated rather than a politics of difference, which could lead to new frameworks and new power relations within institutions such as schools. My first question considers what the new managerialism means for women who take up leadership roles in education. Drawing on data from a large qualitative study of women school leaders in Victoria, Australia, I identify currently available gender scripts. I also outline ways in which these scripts limit possibilities and/or provide opportunities for women who lead in education.

My second question is focused on how feminist researchers need to address the issue of women and leadership within currently available discursive frames. What follows is a discussion of the shortcomings of the study of leadership to date and several suggestions for strategic thinking about women and educational leadership for the future.

Discourses of "new managerialist" theory inform us that diversity is the key to productivity and gaining competitive advantage for nation-states in the more globalized economies of the new millennium (Aburdene and Naisebett

1992; Clarke and Newman 1997, 432). The new managerialism arises out of the material and cultural conditions of globalization, namely, flexible specialization and a shift in orientation from production to consumption. The "soft" strand of the new managerialism reflects the shift from manufacturing to service industries. The "hard" strand of reengineering emphasizes streamlining processes (and people) through the use of new information and communication technologies (Willmott 1995).

Globalization also has produced new occupational and institutional identity crises (Du Gay 1996). The new managerialism requires a sense of belonging and self-actualization, a "postmodern faith" in teamwork and employee empowerment. Nikolas Rose has discussed how, in this new view of managers, economic progress, career progress, and personal development intersect in what he calls a new "psycho-therapeutic territory" (Rose 1992, 115). In this context, visionary leadership comes "from the soul and the market simultaneously" (Clarke and Newman 1997, 429).

## SHIFTS IN DISCOURSE

In the new managerialism, women (and other groups) are viewed as producers and consumers in an increasingly feminized "postmodern" workplace. They are viewed as a force to contend with, or to exploit. A discourse of diversity, which is ultimately assimilationist, prevails. A discourse of difference, which derives from an understanding that difference should be recognized and valued, is muted.

In uncertain deregulated current times, this reflects the "successful" mainstreaming of liberal feminist theory and fosters the exclusion of other more radical feminisms (Blackmore 1996). Whereas the exclusionary practices of "old management" were "the object of fear and loathing for women positioned on its margins, the new managerial discourse is conterminous with both the real (if small) movement of more women in management positions" (Clarke and Newman 1997, 429). A discourse has emerged that justifies such "inclusiveness" and links arguments about how we need more "feminine qualities" in management to arguments that call for a more sensitive approach to people management, an approach that will capture both the hearts and minds of workers. This new discourse of diversity was exemplified in the Australian context by the Karpin Report of the Working Party on Management Education (1995). This report revealed a paradigm shift in leadership, which will mean that more women, and those of non-Anglo background, are likely to be managers in the twenty-first century.

The new discourse of diversity takes a more pluralistic, economistic slant on the liberal democratic discourses that have dominated Western feminist discourses in the past century. In the current market-oriented and client-focused education industry, women are seen both as a new niche market and as a wasted source of leadership talent. This perspective is exemplified by Australia's Women Adviser, appointed by a conservative federal government in 1988, who stated that women cannot expect to get special treatment on the basis of rights and needs. She went on to say that women must illustrate how they can contribute to national productivity. This indicates a significant shift from feminist concerns about rights and needs, concerns that gave women access to the welfare state in the 1970s and 1980s. There has also been a dismantling of the welfare state in favor of a competitive state. That state now abrogates its responsibility for women, as a disadvantaged group, by allowing free play to market forces to become the primary distributive mechanism of social and material goods.

## SHIFTS IN ORGANIZATIONAL THEORY

In organizational theory, the appeal to more feminine styles of leadership is part of the shift from earlier rationalist approaches that "partitioned emotional effort from reward" toward attempts to recapture the emotional lives of employees by developing their commitment to more collaborative and family friendly workplaces (Coates 1997, 430). As the "corporate culture gurus" argued back in the 1980s, people have been the last untapped resource left to add value and thus increase productivity. Organizational theorists who recognized that women and men have different perceptions about organizations and organizational life have sought to realize new possibilities for appropriating feminine modes such as connectedness (Coates 1997). This has resulted in a partial inclusion of women into executive positions, partial in the sense that there is a rapidly revolving door as women enter and exit executive positions rapidly (see further discussion of this in chapter 5 of this book). In this scenario, the hegemonic culture of competitive success remains unchanged, if not exaggerated, as a slash-and-burn approach, or "cowboy" culture of hyped-up, market-oriented organizations, prevails (Kanter 1990). This denies evidence that organizations are highly dependent upon emotions (Fineman 1993; Blackmore 1996). Loyalty, motivation, and satisfaction, as well as fear, are key aspects of organizational success, while the market relies upon envy, desire, pleasure, and greed.

In Australia, there has been a gradual, although erratic, institutionalization of gender equity policies in the workplace as a result of state feminist interventions and feminist activism in the workplace (Eisenstein 1996). This could be seen to indicate the success of equal opportunity policies, yet it is clear that employment equity policies have not achieved their expectations. Women continue to be underrepresented globally in educational leadership and other areas of executive management. There is limited progression, with women increasingly concentrated in the school principalship (at the assistant level, particularly) rather than the superintendency, and in universities, at the level of head of

department or dean rather than as vice chancellors or presidents of universities
(Stromquist 1997). There is deeply embedded "rigid flexibility" despite rhetoric
about level playing fields and flexible workforces.

## SHIFTS IN GLOBAL LABOR PATTERNS

Feminist labor process theorists such as Walby (1997) and Pillinger (1993) pre-
dict a pessimistic scenario that depicts global labor patterns in which most
women continue to be located on the margins of a global workforce polarized
between rich and poor along gender, class, and race lines. Core workers enjoy
secure, well-paid careers, while marginalized workers exist by moving between
numerous casual and underpaid jobs (see further discussion in chapter 4 of this
book). Restructuring has produced a regendering of work, one particularly evident in teaching in many Western liberal capitalist states (Blackmore 1997).
Institutional flexibility in increasingly devolved education systems is contingent
upon workforce flexibility. Teachers become mobile educational out-workers,
capable of moving across a range of educational sites but without the long-term
benefits of employment security, professional development, or a collegial environment. Teaching becomes a "feminized" role, whether it is taken up by men
or women. Institutional leaders, many of them women, are therefore in the
unenviable position of overseeing what many view as the deskilling and depro-
fessionalization of teaching under a new regime of flexibility.

## SHIFTS IN EMPHASIS

Yet another shift in education during this age of the new managerialism is the
rise of market-focused school systems. Earlier social justice discourses have
been replaced by discourses that stress achieving equity by allowing individuals
to exercise choice and to gain access to learning technologies in increasingly
deinstitutionalized learning environments. Organizations must address the specific needs of clients, or those clients will withdraw.

    This, then, is the context in which many women are seeking to practice
what has been called "women's ways of leading." In the remainder of this chapter, I discuss three ways in which feminist researchers need to address the issue
of women and leadership, given the limits of present discursive frames. I
describe some of the gender scripts of leadership that are currently offered and
discuss how these provide limited possibilities for women in current times. I
consider the assumptions about power, change, and difference that are embedded in current scripts. This chapter draws upon data collected from a large qualitative research project in Victoria, Australia, which used a range of methodologies, including unstructured interviews, reflective journals, writing workshops,
and focus groups. While the study is located in Australia, the gender equity dis-

courses revealed similarities to those discussed by theorists in many Western liberal states (Arnot and Weiler 1993) such as New Zealand (Court 1994, 1995), the United Kingdom (Weiner 1995), Canada (Reynolds and Young 1995), and the United States (Schmuck 1996).

## WOMEN LEADERS AS TROUBLE

Women can be seen as trouble because they are, as a group, underrepresented in positions of power and authority (Butler 1990). That observation weakens claims that leadership already is democratic. Feminists in Australia, New Zealand, and Scandinavia have previously relied upon "statecentric equal employment opportunity" claims (Yeatman 1992, 449) to redress the underrepresentation of women in leadership roles. With globalization, however, the state "is now, less a unit of governance with respect to a self-determining citizen community and more a unit of political management with respect to how its internal subjects and their economic activities articulate with transnational markets and institutions" (ibid.). The state, in many Anglophone liberal countries, as a consequence of radical structural adjustment policies, increasingly mediates the market, modifying only its excesses rather than actively intervening in the economy to maintain some level of equality. The state is increasingly less concerned with meeting the citizenship (rights-based) and welfare (needs-based) claims of its members. The market is now the primary distributive mechanism for both social (e.g., welfare, education, and health) and material goods. Indeed, as already discussed in this chapter, the corporatization of the state has facilitated the discursive redefinition of inequality away from needs and rights to that which is earned through the market by "merit" alone, and not through any sense of entitlement, right, or even fairness. This changes how feminists can argue for a greater representation of women in leadership roles.

## WOMEN LEADERS CREATING TROUBLE

Even once women have gained leadership roles, they can be construed as creating trouble. Strong women often are seen as difficult, dangerous, and even deviant, because they "trouble" dominant masculinities and modes of management by being different. This difference can become exaggerated if they exercise a different voice and insist on declaring their femaleness in what were historically male domains. Females who are different can interrupt the tendency in executive management cultures for homo-social reproduction and closure (Sinclair 1994). Feminist leaders can be particularly disruptive, because they frequently try to change organizational cultures and structures as well as individual attitudes in order to achieve more inclusive workplaces and gender justice. Despite this, feminist leaders often have been unable to produce the cultural

and structural shifts expected. This is true in part because gender equity policies, enforced through legislation, have focused more on changing individual
women to better fit the demands of leadership rather than on changing men,
changing notions of leadership, or changing organizations. The success of gender equity reform lies primarily in getting women aspirants and leaders to network, mentor, plan careers, acquire financial skills, and be assertive and entrepreneurial, that is, to work more like corporate men.

Feminism has had little impact on gender power relations, as there has
been little political will to change organizations and, until recently, no will at
all to change men. Within emergent discourses that depict men as victims of
feminism and declare that feminism has gone too far, feminism has been
declared to be trouble (Lingard and Douglas 1999). This has resulted in a
backlash against feminism. Men have called upon the same employment equity discourses that arose out of feminism's demands for equal rights for
women, to position individual men as being disadvantaged. Eveline (1994)
points out, however, that what has been lost is men's systemic advantage. A
new discourse of diversity, which speaks about managing diversity, too readily equates individual preferences to differences produced by such characteristics as race, class, gender, and ethnicity. Managing diversity is reduced to satisfying wants in a therapeutic sense rather than addressing structural and
social inequalities. Difference is constructed as a problem. It is not valued or
seen as a benefit. Backlash discourses position feminists as being opposed to
change when defending past gains. Such discourses water down the language
of justice and position feminists as being anti-reform and out of date. The
notion of change itself becomes problematic, in that good leaders are only
seen as promoting ongoing change, whether or not that change has implications for equity.

## WOMEN LEADERS AS TROUBLE FOR FEMINISM

Women leaders also can be seen to trouble feminism itself. A useful distinction
was made by Chantal Mohanty (1992) when she talked about the difference
between "being feminist" and "being female." She pointed to the volatility of
the category of "woman" itself. I suggest that feminism (as a social movement
and in a disciplinary form of knowledge) has its own normative and regulato-
ry tendencies that we need to constantly review. Powerful feminist expectations
that all women apprise "women's styles of leadership" can build expectations
about leadership that many women, feminist or not, find difficult to achieve
because of the industrial, political, and economic constraints of leadership in
postmodern organizations. Women in formal leadership work within systems
not of their own making, systems that privilege men in general and privilege
certain dominant modes of masculinity (see further discussion of this point in
chapter 6 of this book).

Finally, the issue of women and leadership, I argue in more depth else-where (Blackmore 1999a), has been decontextualized, distorted, and depoliti-cized for six main reasons. The first is due to the emphasis on leadership itself as the linchpin of change. The second is the conflation of "female" with "fem-inist" leadership. The third is the deflection of attention away from focusing upon the relations of gender and therefore the advantages gained through par-ticular dominant masculinities (Brittan 1989). The fourth is from a blindness to the constraints placed upon women leaders by educational restructuring. The fifth is the failure to adequately theorize change. And the sixth is because of a micro-focus rather than a macro-focus taken by poststructural feminism. Parlo Singh (1995, 96) makes this ironic point.

> It seems paradoxical that when capitalism is restructuring the state across national boundaries in new structures of international education, that social educational theorists attempt to avoid political and theoretical impe-rialism by speaking only for the "self."

This absorption with "the self" (Casey 1995) is evident in the literature on women and leadership. There has been significant research focus on the life histories (Reynolds 1987), career paths, and leadership styles of successful women in management, as well as strategies for getting into leadership. However, unlike Reynolds in chapter 2 of this book, most investigations have focused on the underrepresentation of women in leadership positions rather than on the meaning-making processes of women leaders or the influence of context upon their leadership activities. Singh (1995, 196) aptly comments that the research needs to explore the historical interrelationship between various forms of social differentiation. We need to question the similarities and differ-ences of those within the social category "women."

Mainstream discourses continue to construct women as a *problem* for educational leadership rather than problematizing the concept of leadership itself, relative to dominant power and gender relations. There also is the prob-lem of category politics, which Carol Bacchi (1996) suggests has two aspects. First, there is the politics that surround meaning making. Meanings are con-structed and acted upon in terms of particular assumptions. Second, there is the politics of identity, which is about how particular social groups (such as women, blacks, Greeks, etc.) came to see themselves and then make claims for equity. Category politics produces a sense of immutability or fixedness about the category it seeks to define. People come to be seen as belonging in a sin-gle category, such as "black" or "woman." Category politics also leads to blind-ness. It does not recognize what is not categorized or named. Take, for exam-ple, white, middle-class women leaders who do not talk about their "white-ness" or about their class position (Roman 1993). In contrast, black women leaders are frequently positioned as black, working class, and women leaders. The category of "woman" (Riley 1988) has gained a fixedness within gender equity policies, and the categories of race and ethnicity have been treated as subsets. As argued in the previous chapter by Reynolds, we should seek, rather, to think about categories as shifting and changing over time.

The conceptual categories of equal opportunity, affirmative action, equity, and diversity also are problematic. Like the categories of women, race, and ethnicity, these concepts are best viewed as fluid and open to a variety of meanings. Such concepts are important, because they achieve legitimacy through legislation and government funding. These concepts offer possibilities for women but also for other interest groups. The discourse of diversity promises to recognize the benefits of a diverse workplace or school population, but the discourse of diversity, when utilized in a market context, is premised upon the individual's right to choose. The assumption is that equity will be achieved through the exercise of individual choice. This disregards any sense of need or obligation to others as well as ignores material and cultural circumstances that restrict the exercise of "free" choice.

Focusing on administration, as feminists in the field have tended to do, is also conceptually problematic, as it leaves the gender division of labor intact. Administration often is separated from teaching in research and theory (for exceptions, see Weiner 1995; Kenway et al. 1997). Dominant models for administration have remained so intact that particular hegemonic masculinities can be seen to reconstitute themselves over time—whether this has been the patriarchal model of the nineteenth century, the rationalist model of the bureaucratic state, or the multi-skilled corporate manager of the late twentieth century (Blackmore 1999a).

Some feminists, such as those whose work is highlighted in this book, have tried to reconceptualize leadership. They have argued that leadership is practiced by teachers as well as by principals and parents, even when these individuals or their institutions have not named or recognized these activities as leadership. There still exists, however, the embedded assumption that when it comes to leadership, "it takes an extraordinary woman to do what an ordinary man does." This is a myth that has deterred many women from seeking formal leadership roles. Such myths are perpetuated by discourses that circulate about women and leadership. These discourses offer particular gender scripts to women in schools.

## THE GENDER SCRIPTS OF LEADERSHIP

The discourses surrounding women and leadership in new hard times of deregulated markets and economic rationalism are complex and contradictory. Many of the gender scripts of leadership are the products of feminist research and feminism that have taken on particular "populist" readings. The most popular descriptor of good female leadership is about "being strong," in contrast to the tough boy scripts for male leaders (Chase 1995).

## "Being Strong" Script

This script reads that a woman in leadership is expected to show strength in the face of adversity, discrimination, and resistance while maintaining her good nature and "niceness" along the way. Being strong is about standing up against resistance, refusing to give in on matters of principle, and defending the weak. Being strong is equated, in this script, to being in control of one's emotions and not succumbing to taunting or teasing. Being strong is standing up for one's position, no matter what. Being strong is not about being unemotional but rather controlling negative emotions such as anger and frustration. Being strong means that, in a desire to be better teachers and leaders, women should only display the positive emotions of caring and sharing. In addition to these notions of being strong, even more readings are available for women of color and ethnic background. Mirza (1993) points out that being strong for black women means dealing with discrimination, both on the basis of gender and race. Yet there is little discussion of differences among women, or how different women, such as black and white women, may discriminate against one another.

The being strong script is difficult in that women are depicted as needing to be "strong," a highly masculine "physical" descriptor, to succeed as leaders. However, they must be strong in the emotional and moral sense, a highly feminine "emotional" descriptor. Furthermore, the strength of individual women in this script is attributed to their capacity to cope, survive, and even flourish in the face of discrimination and adversity. This implies that women, through their experiences of subordination, are made strong by that very subordination (Mirza 1993). This is a strategically dangerous position, because it implies that good leaders can be made from a discriminatory system!

Finally, being strong requires women to sublimate that emotional aspect of leadership for which women have been seen to be special: no tears, just passion and courage, as described by Strachan's feminist leaders in chapter 6. Strong women leaders are expected to be good role models, mentors, and advocates for other women. They are to do this all without complaint or recognition of the pressure that they themselves are under. Strong women are expected to be able to mount arguments for all women, at any time, on request. This poses two challenges. First, these women are expected to take it on the chin when their focus is not seen as working for the general good. Second, these women are subject to harsh criticism by other feminists in the "strong, albeit contested, current within feminism. This current holds that speaking for others is arrogant, vain, unethical, and politically illegitimate" (Alcoff 1991, 17). These two challenges can lead to a retreat response in women.

> [T]his response is simply to retreat from all practices of speaking forth and assert that one can only know one's own narrow individual experience and one's own truth and never make claims beyond this. This response is

motivated in part by the desire to recognise difference, for example, different priorities, without organising these differences into hierarchies. (Alcoff 1991, 17)

## "SUPERWOMAN" SCRIPT

The Superwoman script is visible when women are heralded in the media as being equally successful mothers, wives, daughters, leaders, and community workers. Superwomen are all things to all people. Such a discourse, while positioning particular individual women as powerful on all fronts, tends to ignore the personal costs that such Superwoman behavior requires. It also often discourages women aspirants, because they feel incapable of playing the Superwoman role. Superwomen are often harshly criticized when they shift the balance and, at some moment, put family before job, exit work altogether, or set up their own business. These are some of the responses that arise from overwork or the stress of working in the chilly climate of large organizations (Cox 1996, 93–94). Strategically, feminists have recognized the burden of the double shift of work and home. They have argued, through their unions and industrial relations reform, for more family friendly workplaces. On the home front, they have sought to negotiate a redistribution of domestic labor to husbands or, when that fails, to domestic help. Such support allows fuller participation in the corporate lifestyle, but it also offers up women to be sacrificed to the "greedy organization" so that they can work longer and harder.

## "CHOOSING LEADERSHIP OVER LOVE" SCRIPT

There is an age-old script about women who choose leadership over love. These women are seen to have made considerable personal sacrifices to get into leadership by choosing work over family and social life. This is substantiated, even in contemporary times, by the profiles of women principals, most of whom continue to be single, divorced, or married without dependent children. This is illustrated by some of the women described by Reynolds in the previous chapter. This script harks back to that of the teacher spinster of the nineteenth century who was nourished in her femininity by vicariously gaining a sense of the maternal through caring for other women's children, and, as in the nineteenth century, this discourse of sacrifice has a downside. The single woman's sexuality is often queried, particularly if she is overtly feminist, as feminism outside of a heterosexual relationship often is read to mean lesbianism (Blount 1996). Nor do such women receive much feminist sympathy, as they are viewed as privileged because they have both seniority and mobility, not having exited the workforce at any time for child rearing or not having been tied down by children's or partner's demands. Indeed, they are often perceived to be dangerous competitors with an unfair advantage, given that occupational success is so contingent upon mobility.

## "POSTMODERNIST" SCRIPT

There also is a postmodernist script that characterizes women as good change agents in organizations. Women are seen to be more flexible and to cope with change better than their male colleagues (Court 1994). Women leaders are both insiders and outsiders in male-dominated management, and as such they are cognizant of the values, practices, and workings of management. But they also are outside of the male networks, marginal to the dominant cultures and with less self-interest in the status quo, given their marginalization. As "outsiders inside," they are in a position of advantage, readily cast as a change agent (Eisenstein 1996; Cox 1996; Yeatman 1992). Their power is derived from their difference, their capacities as women to facilitate change. This script was explained by some of the women in Reynold's previous chapter as "having bought our own fate." Collegial networks outside of the system or among women in similar situations provide women who are playing out this script with support and strategic advice on how to survive as the loner. But their difference and change agentry is valued in the organization only to the extent that these women can meet such demands within organizationally defined parameters. Quite often, women are appointed on the basis of their community links and credibility, as is the case for many Aboriginal women principals and leaders in Australia. They are therefore failures or perceived to be trouble when they do not conform to organizational rules, but they are seen to be disloyal by their communities when they do (Ngurruwutthun and Stewart 1996). To step outside of the organization's parameters means being too political and attuned to community. Such women are expendable once the task is achieved or if they have not met the high expectations laid upon them. Being a change agent is difficult and dangerous work.

## "WOMEN'S STYLES OF LEADERSHIP" SCRIPT

Another popular script highlights women's "special contribution" by bringing to organizations a "women's style of leadership." Women are seen to be a new source of leadership talent because of their caring and sharing propensities, their communicative and organizational skills, and their capacity to listen to and empathize with the needs of others. These traits are deemed critical to new managerialism in postmodern organizations, because value adding is gained through person productivity (Beck 1994). The inclusion of female characteristics into leadership means that all leaders can be expected to call upon the full spectrum of human behaviors (Weiner 1995). In the Karpin Report (1995), for example, the "new" manager of the twenty-first century was depicted as most likely to be female because of the new person-oriented demands being placed on managers due to globalization. The Karpin Report argued that, "Major improvements in management skills can be effected simply by opening up equal opportunities" (xix). It stated that, "The role of women in society has

meant many of them have already developed some of the soft skills that are critical for the future" (126). Hard skills were described by Karpin as being associated with traditional strategies. Soft skills, however, were described as involving
motivating staff, creating cooperation, redefining organizational values and
beliefs, and realigning management focus. A senior manager will require the
additional range of soft skills in a capabilities-based organization.

Another more problematic reductionist and conservative reading of the
discourse of women's styles of leadership is that men and women are irrecon-
cilably different and that the differences are complementary. This is no
advancement from the position that many first-wave feminists made in the late
1890s, when they demanded access to equal pay and to leadership positions in
girl's schools (Blackmore 1999a). These readings tend to maintain the fixedness
of the category of gender rather than making it fluid. In so doing, they reduce
the possibilities for transforming the social relations of gender. The discourse of
the collective has also meant that any highlighting of differences among women
or criticisms of women in leadership, by other women, is viewed as disloyal and
subversive of the feminist principle of valuing women. This is evident in the
difficulties that women have at the institutional and interpersonal levels in dealing with peer relationships, when in positions of power and authority. It also is
evident in the difficulties that women have in negotiating the territory between
powerful and less powerful women and in trying to mediate differences based
on age, experience, organization power, and political beliefs (Schmuck 1996;
Cox 1996).

Feminist research on women in leadership provides evidence that *many*
women principals are more caring, collaborative, communicative, consultative,
communitarian, consensus oriented, and student and curriculum focused. This
research has the tendency to produce a regime of truth that *all* women leaders
are caring and sharing, which is of course highly problematic. The discourses of
women's ways of seeing, doing, knowing, organizing, and leading are ones that
have been powerful for women in the 1980s in that they imply a collective
practice that offers an alternative position to hegemonic and masculinist discourses about leadership. There is, however, significant conflation between
"being female" and "being feminist," which leads to what Chantal Mohanty
calls the feminist osmosis thesis.

> Being female is thus seen as naturally related to being feminist, where the
> experience of being female transforms women into feminists through
> osmosis. Feminism is not defined as a highly contested political terrain; it
> is the mere effect of being female. (Mohanty 1992, 77)

The collapse of any distinction between "female" and "feminist" leadership has significant consequences for gender equity. It does not always contribute to productive thinking about feminist theories of practice, in that it
reduces to idealizing a particular approach to which women only can adhere,

or for which women only are responsible (i.e., more democratic and support-
ive educational organizations). Nor does it address the social relations of gender as hegemonic masculinity remains unreconstructed and the norm that
women (or so-called women's skills) complement. Furthermore, it ignores
political differences among women and provides considerable scope for its
appropriation by nonfeminist women who benefit from such a discourse without sacrificing for the sisterhood. Finally, it does not address the issue of values
or politics. It ignores the political project of feminism about producing greater
structural and social equality. All of the above scripts revisit the old differ-
ence/sameness binaries; that is, being different from or the same as men. Such
binaries divert attention away from the issue of power and representation.

## "Power" Script

This script positions women as powerful and arises out of the shared cultural
experience and attributes of being female: women's shared ways of seeing,
being, and doing, the collectivity of experiencing women's culture and knowledge (Belenky et al. 1986). For feminists, it invokes a positive view of power
and how power can be used in creative ways for women, in that women are
powerful in their own terms. Strategic interventions developing out of this
position, therefore, include the development of women-centered knowledge
about leadership, women-only professional development, women-friendly
environments, gender-inclusive leadership, and a range of programs seeking to
raise women's self-esteem, skills, and aspirations. The aim is to impart full and
equal recognition to women's collective experience. Here power is "productive," not just repressive; it is a form of creative energy. This view is similar to
many of the women described by Hall in chapter 1 of this book. The corollary,
of course, is that men too could become fuller human beings by increasing
their repertoire of social skills, and they could become more compassionate and
caring. Many of the women interviewed in my research projects did not name
themselves as feminist, because they felt being feminist was too political and
confrontational. However, nearly all appealed to the popularized feminist discourses, as does Karpin (1995) about women's styles of leadership as being caring and sharing. They also promoted the popular "critical mass theory" that
suggests that more women in leadership will transform the male culture of
management. Some readings of the power script, however, reduce the complex
and substantive philosophical, moral, and political feminist arguments and
empirical evidence concerning an ethic of care (Noddings 1992). In the previous chapter, Reynolds argues against such a reduction and offers a complex
view of how morality and gender relations are related and how these are resistant to change over time. The popular reading appropriated in the management
literature, however, tends to reduce an ethic of care to a matter of technique
that can be readily acquired by anyone, regardless of their political persuasion.

Such is the case for skills of interpersonal relations, consultation, and communication (Weiner 1995). Kerfoot and Knights (1993) suggest that popular readings concerning care allow sensitive new age guys (SNAGS) to earn organizational brownie points through the public display of parenting (e.g., taking kids to work or to the playground), while there has been no actual revaluing of domestic labor due to a fairer distribution (i.e., women are home cleaning the toilet). In so doing, men may gain a competitive advantage over women with a sympathy vote for being pro-feminist and over all other men who are seen to be recalcitrant, macho males.

## "Professional Success" Script

All of the aforementioned scripts coexist in the same organizational narratives with another script, that of professional success. In this script, the success of individual women is due to hard work, merit, and sheer professionalism alone. Susan Chase (1995) found that in the United States, "Women superintendents embrace their professional competencies and success and develop a primary commitment to their professional work . . . a narrative of the successful, ambitious woman has achieved a certain substance" (10). This is the ultimate expression of the twentieth-century administrative paradigm of bureaucratic rationality. It also is liberalism's notion of the freely operating, gender-neutral individual who makes choices. Such a person achieves leadership through her capacities as an individual, not as a woman. It is a favorable image in the competitive culture of the education market, one that is seductive to younger women who think that gender equality has been achieved. This new professionalism focuses on technical expertise that can be purchased by anyone rather than the twentieth-century notion of professionalism involving some sense of public trusteeship and advocacy. This new professionalism reinforces the sense of gender neutrality (evidenced in some of those studied in Reynolds' previous chapter) and therefore is not necessarily a safe space for feminists to occupy.

## "Social Male" Script

Closely associated with the "professional success" script is the less talked about script of the "social male." The social male script is taken on by women who are seen by their feminist colleagues to assume the worst attributes of the male norms of hard-core masculinist leadership. While many women principals disclaim feminism, others are distinctly anti-feminist (Weiner 1995). These social males often are described by colleagues as being aggressive, dominant, competitive, individualistic, and nonsupportive, if not outright antagonistic to other women. They often gather men around them, once in leadership, to the exclusion of other women. Being the only female, but also not "one of the boys," these women are offered differential treatment and status as "the exception." They take no responsibility to assist, encourage, or mentor other women, as they feel that they made it themselves, based on their own effort and merit, and thus they expect other women to do the same.

Feminists confront significant dilemmas about how to respond to such women. Feminist discourses about the collective have bred some reluctance among feminists regarding the criticism of women leaders. Such solidarity often is misplaced, however, as it ignores personal differences among women. The feminist osmosis thesis already discussed in this chapter can work to undermine strategic thinking about how to better theorize change in gender relations.

## STRATEGIC THINKING FOR THE FUTURE

Strategically, I am suggesting that, while the women's "styles of leadership" discourse has been empowering for many women, it also can be dangerous. Its hegemony can lead to introspectivity and lack of reflexivity, which produces a new meta-narrative about the category "women." The downside to this is that the reification of caring and sharing can be a guilt trap for women teachers and women principals. This guilt trap is described by Sandra Acker (1995), who suggests that women put children's or others' welfare first and their own welfare second, a sentiment expressed by some of the women described by Reynolds in the previous chapter. This guilt trap also can lead to compliance and not change agentry, reaction rather than pro-action. The feminist osmosis thesis I have described in this chapter not only fails to address the contingent nature of subjectivity and identity formation of women in leadership, it also reifies particular ways of leading without regard for the context or substance of leadership. Most of these leadership scripts I have described here fail to address the personal costs of leadership and the complexity of being female, being feminist, and being a leader. They also present women as a homogeneous category and, in so doing, they reify gender difference and deny racial, cultural, and political differences among women. They do not challenge the dominant male norm, because they leave the masculine/feminine dualism untouched. To break this bind, we have to make a number of significant shifts.

First, we need to move beyond the dualistic position that still remains embedded in feminist research in educational administration. This means focusing on the social relations of gender, and not just women in leadership. We need to make masculinity problematic. This shift has already occurred within the literature on the education of girls (see, e.g., Kenway et al. 1997). Much of the new sociology of masculinity that focuses on boys is being informed by pro-feminist male researchers, and they are likely allies with feminists in arguments against hegemonic masculinities in management, as men too are often excluded (Connell 1995; Lingard and Douglas 1999). Just as women leaders have been provided with a limited range of scripts, so too, as Reynolds argued in chapter 2, have men. There has been one dominant script for men and leadership that has the appearance of some "trans-historical essence"—that of the aggressive, rational, strong leader, capable of making the hard decisions. The fragility and irrationality underpinning this enduring image of hegemonic masculinity is denied, largely because most men benefit from its maintenance, even though it does not correspond to the reality of most men. This image also excludes women. To focus upon masculinity gives feminists the scope to undermine the dualisms embedded in educational administration.

Second, the co-optation of feminist discourses about leadership for diversity arises out of specific material and economic conditions arising from globalization and the new work order of postindustrial society (Morrison 1992). Masculinity and femininity are being reconstituted in relation to each other, a critical aspect of the changing nature of work for postmodern "globalized" economies (Blackmore 1999b). Again, there is significant disjunction between the discourses of leadership, which are seen to be desirable at this moment, and the fundamental restructuring of the workforce, which is affecting realities for many women administrators and teachers. The most optimistic scenario emphasizes fluidity, flexibility, teamwork, flatter organizations, localized decision making, multi-skilling, and professional autonomy. This scenario is premised on rhetorics about learning organizations, learning cities, and lifelong learning. It is one in which education is perceived as a critical investment. This is a discourse that holds promise for women, one we have to promote actively as educators and feminists and one that provides an alternative to economically driven approaches to globalization.

There are warning signs, however, that the potential for affirmative restructuring has not been achieved. The growth of credentialism, narrowing conceptualizations of administration, and new regimes of appraisal, selection, and development are among these warning signs. In the desire for greater control in a deregulated and devolved workplace, new technologies of surveillance and accountability have emerged that focus on quantifiable outcomes, raw scores, performance indicators, and performance management. In the short term, feminists have to work at the institutional level to tap into these new technologies and to push for equity. They have to be included as central to performance indicators, quality assurance processes, and outcomes-based learning. In the long term, feminists need to seek a more balanced understanding of the nature of quality teaching and learning beyond that which can be quantified and measured.

A third shift also needs to take place. While the various leadership scripts described in this chapter highlight image, style, and process, there is little reference to substance. We need to ask what we are leading for. Leadership in postmodern times is increasingly about image management, about portraying schools or universities as living up to, if not setting, the "best practice." Leaders are expected to mirror the image of their schools, and educational leadership is increasingly about being in a "constant state of visibility" (Bartky 1990, 65). From outside the organization, leadership often is reduced to just "being strong" or "entrepreneurial," to making decisions rather than determining how one can promote one's school (and one's self) without losing a sense of the public good. On the outside, it is spoken of as "marketing character": "I am as you desire me" (Fromm 1979). Women principals talk about "re-making" themselves on a daily basis, deciding which woman they are going to be today. On the inside, however, image management puts significant pressure on educational leaders to manage risk, control uncertainty, and downplay dissension (Blackmore 1996). This counters the evidence on successful educational change that focuses on improving student outcomes, the quality of the learning experience, and the well-being of students and teachers. The assumption in the literature is that "good" educational leadership is about encouraging debate, being open to new ideas, utilizing a range of strategies and techniques, and supporting innovation and risk taking.

A fourth significant shift that needs to take place is that feminists have to challenge the assumption that the market is a viable alternative to the state as the distributive mechanism of social goods. The market, it is suggested, will cater for diversity but more often produces a narrow range of images about what constitutes good leaders, good schools, and good universities (Gerwitz et al. 1995). Education markets where educational institutions compete for "clients," where parental choice of schools is exercised, and where the media is an increasingly important player do not promote diversity. Markets more often demand a display of educational goods through an expanding array of performance indicators, standardized test scores, and international benchmarks. These have a normalizing effect and are the other side of the privatization of public education. The privatization debate over substantive educational issues takes such issues as the feminization of poverty and youth unemployment outside of the organization to the public. In times of "strong corporate cultures," participants in such debates can be equated to dissension and disloyalty. The pressure on individual feminist women leaders to conform to corporate values is great.

New managerialism, with its postmodernist focus on flexibility, still maintains a strongly anti-statist and anti-social engineering stance. It rejects the role of a strongly interventionist state (particularly in the area of employment equity or affirmative action), because it reduces competition and argues for self-regulation. Employment equity and affirmative action also are seen to disrupt the "natural selection" processes of the market which, it is argued, will reward merit, if appropriately packaged. Women are thus caught between state and market where conservative economic orthodoxies define the state as bad and the market as good. Historically, equity has been delivered by the state and not by the market. Organizations, as nation-states, dampen down women's demands for the conditions that make full participation possible (e.g., child care, flexible hours, permanent part-time work, job sharing) on the grounds that they undermine the organization's or state's comparative advantage. Equity is too costly in globalized economies.

Finally, the management literature has an ongoing denial of the embedded structural inequalities that exist inherently in educational organizations and the market. It does not matter whether one talks about the empowerment of workers or the enhancement of work through the use of new technologies. The new managerialism adheres to a form of "instrumental humanism" that treats diversity as another resource to be exploited (Willmott 1995; Morrison 1992). Feminist discourses of teamwork and communication are ripe for the picking, too readily appropriated, and subsumed without regard for the analysis of structural inequality and different value systems that underpin their origins. The appropriation of feminist discourses typifies social commentaries about the superficiality of the nature of the postmodern "therapeutic" state, a state where multiculturalism and diversity conjure up images of the exotic and desirable, something to be tasted, without having to deal with the cultural processes leading to their production. Likewise, feminism is to be consumed, enjoyed, and indulged in without having to understand the range of moral, political, and ethical imperatives underpinning its origins and the responsibilities and obligations entailed with regard to its defense. The discourse of diversity is increasingly about the "democratization of self esteem" that operates at a surface level of consumption. As Lasch (1995) puts it, "The current catchwords—diversity, compassion, empowerment, entitlement—express the wistful hope that deep divisions in American society can be bridged by goodwill and sanitized speech" (7).

Leadership in this context is increasingly being treated as a skill and a competence. It is not about articulating and advocating arguments that call upon a range of personal, political, intellectual, and ethical value positions. Leadership has been depoliticized at the very moment that education is linked to the economy in highly political ways. The paradox is that postmodern discourses of reform require schools to respond reactively to pressing external social demands. Some of these demands are evident in the changed labor market, new technologies, globalization, multiculturalism and, indeed, the megatrends for women to produce new consumers (Aburdene and Naisebett 1992). Education is positioned as reactive rather than as a site that is pro-active in the formation of active citizens who have a sense of tolerance, trust, and respect for difference. The discourses of restructuring have called upon the more optimistic accounts—managing diversity, teamwork, quality, autonomy, flexibility, workplace autonomy, and localized decision making. While these accounts are quite appealing to many feminist sentiments about desirable social and organizational practices, the reality has been a shift toward management prerogative rather than democratic empowerment. This discourse leads to a more managed self rather than self-governance. It also requires that leaders in education be held accountable for outcomes without the material resources to deliver quality education.

## REFERENCES

Aburdene, P., and J. Naisebett. 1992. *Megatrends for Women: From Liberation to Leadership*. New York: Fawcett Columbine.

Acker, S. 1995. "'Carry on Caring': The Work of Women Teachers." *British Journal of Sociology of Education* 16:1:21–36.

Alcoff, L. 1991. "The Problem of Speaking for Others." *Cultural critique* 20:5–33.

Arnot, M., and K. Weiler, eds. 1993. *Feminism and Social Justice: An International Perspective*. London: Falmer Press.

Bacchi, C. 1996. *The Politics of Affirmative Action: Women, Equality, and Category Politics*. London: Sage.

Bartky, S. L. 1990. *Femininity and Domination*. London: Routledge.

Beck, L. 1994. *Reclaiming Educational Administration As a Caring Profession*. New York and London: Teachers College Press.

Belenky, M., B. Clinchy, N. Goldberger, and J. Tarul, eds. 1986. *Women's Ways of Knowing: The Development of Self, Voice, and Mind*. New York: Basic Books.

Blackmore, J. 1996. "Doing Emotional Labor in the Educational Market Place: Stories from the Field of Women in Management." *Discourse* 17:3:337–52.

Blackmore, J. 1997. "Level Playing Field? Feminist Observations of Global/Local Articulations of the Restructuring and Regendering of Educational Work." *International Review of Education* 43:5–6:1–23.

Blackmore, J. 1999a. *Troubling Women: Feminism, Leadership, and Educational Change*. Buckingham: Open University Press.

Blackmore, J. 1999b. "Globalization/Localization: Strategic Dilemmas for State Feminism and Gender Equity Policy." *Special Issue on Globalization and Education—Journal of Education Policy* 14:1:35–54.

Blount, J. 1996. Manly Men and Womanly Women: Deviance, Gender Role Polarization, and the Shift in Women's School Employment 1900–1996. *Harvard Educational Review* 66:2:318–38.

Brittan, A. 1989. *Masculinity and Power*. Oxford and New York: Basil Blackwell.

Butler, J. 1990. *Gender Trouble: Feminism and the Subversion of Identity*. London: Routledge.

Casey, C. 1995. *Work, Self, and Society: After Industrialism*. London: Routledge.

Chase, S. 1995. *Ambiguous Empowerment: The Work Narratives of Women School Superintendents*. Amherst: Massachusetts University Press.

Clarke, J., and J. Newman. 1997. "The Right to Manage: A Second Managerial Revolution?" *Cultural Studies* 7:3:427–41.

Coates, G. 1997. "Organization Men, Women, and Organizational Culture." *Sociological Research Online* 2:3:7 <http://www.socresonline.org.uk/ socresonline/2/3/7. html>.

Connell, R. W. 1995. *Masculinities*. Sydney: Allen & Unwin.

Court, M. 1994. "Removing Macho Management: Lessons from the Field of Education." *Gender, Work, and Organization* 1:1:33–49.

Court, M. 1995. "'Good Girls and Naughty Girls': Rewriting the Scripts for Women's Anger." Pp. 162–73 in *Gender and Changing Educational Management*, ed. B. Limerick, and B. Lingard. Sydney: Hodder and Stoughton.

Cox, E. 1996. *Leading Women: Tactics for Making the Difference*. Sydney: Random House.

Du Gay, P. 1996. *Consumption and Identity at Work*. Newbury Park, Calif.: Sage.

Eisenstein, H. 1996. *Inside Agitators: Australian Femocrats and the State*. St. Leonards: Allen & Unwin.

Eveline, J. 1994. "The Politics of Advantage." *Australian Feminist Studies* 19 (autumn):129–54.

Fineman, S. 1993. "Organizations As Emotional Arenas." Pp. 9–35 in *Emotion in Organizations*, ed. S. Fineman. London: Sage.

Fromm, E. 1979. *To Have or To Be?* London: Abacus.

Gerwitz, S., S. Ball, and R. Bowe. 1995. *Markets, Choice, and Equity in Education*. Buckingham: Open University Press.

Kanter. R. M. 1990. *When Giants Learn to Dance: Mastering the Challenges of Strategy, Management, and Careers in the 1990s*. London: Unwin Hyman.

Karpin Report. 1995. *Enterprising Nation: Ministerial Working Party on Management Education*. Canberra: Australian Government Printing Service.

Kenway, J., and S. Willis, with J. Blackmore, and L. Rennie. 1997. *Answering Back: Girls, Boys, and Feminism in Schools*. Sydney: Allen & Unwin.

Kerfoot, D., and D. Knights. 1993. "Management, Masculinity, and Manipulation: From Paternalism to Corporate Strategy in Financial Services in Britain." *Journal of Management Studies* 30:4:659–77.

Lasch , C. 1995. *The Revolt of the Elites*. New York: W. W. Norton.

Lingard, B., and P. Douglas. 1999. *Men Engaging Feminisms: Profeminism, Backlashes, and Schooling*. Buckingham: Open University Press.

Mirza, H. 1993. "The Social Construction of Black Womanhood in British Educational Research: Towards a New Understanding." Pp. 31–45 in *Feminism and Social Justice*, ed. M. Arnot and K. Weiler. London: Falmer Press.

Mohanty, C. 1992. "Feminist Encounters: Locating the Politics of Experience." Pp. 29–42 in *Destabilizing Theory: Contemporary Feminist Debates*, ed. M. Barrett and A. Phillips. Cambridge, U.K.: Polity Press.

Morrison, A. 1992. *The New Leaders: Guidelines on Leadership Diversity in America*. San Francisco: Jossey-Bass.

Ngurruwutthun N., and M. P. A. Stewart. 1996. "'Learning to Walk Behind; Learning to Walk in Front': A Case Study of the Mentor Program at Yirrkala Community Education Center." *Unicorn* 22:4:3–23.

Noddings, N. 1992. *The Challenge to Care in Schools: An Alternative Approach to Education*. New York: Teachers College Press.

Pillinger, J. 1993. *Feminizing the Market*. Basingstoke: Macmillan.

Reynolds, C. 1987. "Naming the Experience: Women, Men, and Their Changing Worklives As Teachers and Principals." Unpublished doctoral dissertation, University of Toronto.

Reynolds, C., and B. Young, eds. 1995. *Women and Leadership in Canadian Education*. Calgary: Temeron Books.

Riley, D. 1988. *Am I That Name? Feminism and the Category of "Women" in History*. Minneapolis: University of Minnesota Press.

Roman, L. 1993. "White Is a Color! White Defensiveness, Postmodernism, and Anti-Racist Pedagogy." Pp. 71–88 in *Race, Identity, and Representation Education*, ed. C. McCarthy and W. Crichlow. New York and London: Routledge.

Rose, N. 1992. *The Governing of the Soul*. Newbury Park, Calif.: Sage.

Schmuck, P. 1996. "Women's Place in Educational Administration: Past, Present, and Future." Pp. 337–67 in *International Handbook of Educational Leadership and Administration*, ed. K. Leithwood et al. Netherlands: Kluwer Academic Press.

Sinclair, A. 1994. *Trials at the Top: Chief Executives Talk about Men, Women, and the Australian Executive Culture*. Melbourne: Melbourne Business School.

Singh, P. 1995. "Voicing the 'Other', Speaking for the 'Self': Disrupting the Meta-Narratives of Educational Theorizing with Post-Structural Feminisms." Pp. 182–205 in *After Postmodernism*, ed. P. Wexler. London and Washington: Falmer Press.

Stromquist, N. 1997. "Gender Policies in American Education." Pp. 54–72 in *Feminist Critical Policy Analysis*, vol. 1, ed. C. Marshall. London and Washington: Falmer Press.

Walby, S. 1997. *Gender Transformations*. London: Routledge.

Weiner, G. 1995. *Feminism and Education*. Buckingham: Open University Press.

Willmott, H. 1995. "The Odd Couple? Re-engineering Business Processes: Managing Human Resources." *New Technology, Work, and Employment* 10:2:89–98.

Yeatman, A. 1992. "Women's Citizenship Claims: Labor Market Policy and Globalization." *Australian Journal of Political Science* 27:449–61.

# PART II

---

# EXPLORING BEHIND THE STATISTICS: WOMEN'S EXPERIENCES AT THE EDGE OF CHANGE

Statistical profiles on women in leadership roles in schools in a number of Western nations reveal that, while the percentages of women in elementary schools who take on the roles of principal and vice principal have increased over the last few decades, participation rates in secondary schools are still relatively low. In some regions, women have actually lost ground in roles such as the superintendency. In colleges and universities, while the overall number of female faculty members may have increased, the participation of women in roles such as deans or presidents remains low.

The three chapters in this section use statistical analyses and then case studies to look at realities for some particular women educational leaders today in Canada, the United States, and New Zealand. Authors examine the micro impact of macro trends. The chapters investigate some specific experiences of women leaders as they strive to transform their institutions and foster an agenda for increased social justice in school and university settings in their respective countries. In each chapter of this section, women's leadership work in schools is seen in light of their other work as members of families and communities. The reactions of others to the work of women leaders are highlighted. The impact of changing contexts, described in the first section of this book, is described here by delineating the details of decisions regarding leadership made by some individual women.

The last two chapters in this section focus on a small number of women in order to offer rich details of women leaders' experiences in particular settings. This in-depth consideration of the thoughts and feelings of individual women who held "transforming agendas" for the schools in which they were appointed as official leaders reveals commonalities and differences between women in each study and across the two studies, contributing to our understanding of the phenomenon of leadership. This can help us formulate theories about leadership in schools.

In chapter 4, *The "Alberta Advantage": "DeKleining" Career Prospects for Women Educators*, Beth Young points to the difficulty of doing research on women in education when data are not available by sex. Drawing on her study of career patterns for teachers in elementary and secondary schools in Alberta, Canada, where Premier Ralph Klein and his conservative government have fostered a restructuring of public schools, she illustrates two trends for women. The first is an actual decrease in women's participation in central office roles such as the superintendency, and the second is the growing percentage of female teachers that opts for part-time employment.

Young's description of the political environment in present-day Alberta in many ways mirrors the historical scene that Reynolds describes in chapter 2 for another Canadian province, Ontario. There also are strong resemblances between these descriptions and what we hear in Blackmore's chapter 3 and Kenway's and Langmead's chapter 7 about current contexts in Australia. Young argues that the climate of large-scale, government-mandated reform is part of a larger agenda to downsize public spending on services such as schools. This climate continues to construct gender differences, while at the same time it denies those differences and supports the assumption that current policies favor women over men.

Young's chapter shows that records that do exist in Alberta confirm Blackmore's claim in chapter 3, that "restructuring has produced a regendering of work" in schools. That regendering of work in the present Alberta context means that fewer women are reaching the highest levels in school leadership, and more women teachers are working part time. Each of these trends positions women less and less as "core" members of the school organization and more and more as marginalized members of the pool of workers.

In chapter 4, Young offers several explanations for the patterns she observes and draws on an international body of literature to support her views. She ends the chapter by posing several questions that she claims are old but new again. She urges us to continue to work to acknowledge rather than deny gender differences as a factor affecting limits to opportunities in educational organizations and their relation to larger trends in the social setting.

In chapter 5, *Women Administrators and the Point of Exit: Collision between the Person and the Institution*, Patricia Schmuck, Sandra Hollingsworth, and Robyn Lock point to a gap in the women and leadership literature in terms of studies of women who leave leadership roles in education, either voluntarily or involuntarily. Like Strachan (chapter 6), the researchers draw upon a small number of case studies of women leaders, women who are at the cutting edge of change in schools.

Chapter 5 focuses on the context of higher educational institutions, colleges, and universities in the United States at the present time. The limited participation of women in administrative roles in that context is described, and some explanations for this are put forward using the details of four case studies. Each of the women presented in chapter 5 is described as holding a transformative vision for her institution but "identified differently along a feminist continuum." While their goals were reached, eventually they exited from the organization when "their visions collided with purposes of the larger institution." The stories of the experiences of President Janely, Dean Hood, Chair Thomas, and Professor Nippon reveal how individual women came to terms with a gendered politics in an academic setting that problematized efforts to deal with such issues as inclusivity and democracy, equity and diversity, and collectivism and cooperation.

Schmuck, Hollingsworth, and Lock end the chapter with a list of lessons learned from the case studies. These lessons are very useful for anyone who wishes to take up a feminist agenda in a similar environment in whatever country that might be.

In chapter 6, *Feminist Educational Leadership: Not for the Fainthearted*, Jane Strachan from New Zealand argues for the importance of studying micro levels while remaining cognizant of macro-level factors such as the political and social climate of the time and place. In this way, her work is similar to many of the other chapters in this book. Strachan wonders about some of the shortcomings of feminist approaches that have placed heavy burdens of "sainthood" on women leaders. In line with Hall in chapter 1, Strachan argues that school leaders must be expected to be capable of exhibiting the full range of human behavior from the best to the worst.

Chapter 6 presents accounts of how three women leaders in the New Zealand climate of what Strachan describes as "neo-liberal managerialism" tried to accomplish the ideal of a feminist educational leadership committed to working for social justice, sharing power, focusing on care, and emphasizing quality education for students—a tall order indeed! Strachan describes the particulars of the current New Zealand situation in elementary and secondary publicly funded schools, and her account shows many similarities to what has already been described for different contexts in previous chapters. One area of difference, however, centers around her report of the situation with regard to ethnic minority students, including the Pacific Islanders and Maori populations. The three women who Strachan studied, unlike those studied by Hall and discussed in chapter 1, all identified themselves as feminists. Strachan reports differences in the contexts in which these three women carried out their feminist leadership. She describes in detail one principal's commitment to anti-violence, another's advocacy for "at risk" students, and still another's focus on collaborative decision making.

Strachan's chapter presents many of the problems that these three women leaders encountered, but it also describes their successful attempts to enact change, as well as to win the respect and support of most staff and parents. She ends the chapter by asking about the alternative to being "an assertive uppity woman."

CHAPTER FOUR


# THE "ALBERTA ADVANTAGE": "DEKLEINING" CAREER PROSPECTS FOR WOMEN EDUCATORS


Beth Young

*Canada*


## INTRODUCTION

In this chapter, I draw upon statistics from a number of Canadian sources, including my own studies, to investigate patterns in women's participation in teaching and administrative roles in elementary and secondary school systems in Alberta, Canada. There are many ways in which the province of Alberta has served as the Canadian "beachhead" for many reform initiatives in education in the 1980s and 1990s (Kachur and Harrison 1999). These reforms have been similar to those adopted in countries such as New Zealand, Britain, Australia, and parts of the United States over the same time period. My first question therefore is: How have women educators in Alberta been faring during this

Funding for the various studies from which data have been drawn for this chapter has been provided by the Alberta Advisory Committee for Educational Studies, the Support for the Advancement of Scholarship Fund, the Faculty of Education, the University of Alberta, the Alberta Teachers' Association, and the Social Sciences and Humanities Research Council of Canada.

I appreciate not only the funding but the considerable assistance provided by graduate students Hilary Gray, Susan Ansara, Mary Brooks, Cheryl Alexander, and Kathy Grieve.

period of restructuring? As the title of the chapter indicates, I want to know if women in education are enjoying the "Alberta Advantage"[1] touted by Ralph Klein's Conservative government.

My second question grows out of my attempts to gather statistics on women in education and asks why some sectors in school systems have failed to include sex as an important variable for data collection and maintenance. That failure has masked some disturbing shifts that I was able to see in the limited data I found. One trend relates to women's increased participation in administrative roles such as elementary vice principal, and their continued absence from roles such as the school superintendent. Another trend relates to women's participation in increased forms of "part-time" rather than full-time teaching employment. Both trends raise questions similar to those spoken of by Blackmore in chapter 3, concerning core and marginal workers within educational systems today.

The information and discussion in this chapter suggest that women in the current Alberta context are making career decisions that allow them to "get on" with what they wish to do in schools, as do the women described by Hall in chapter 1. Many are coping with restructuring and its fallout. But are these women just making idiosyncratic, individual choices? As Reynolds asks in chapter 2, how does the history of gender relations in schools inform our views about school leadership? I argue that the trends I describe in this chapter demonstrate how women's careers and work lives in schools continue to be constructed according to traditional views of gender roles, even while this process is being denied.

What follows is an attempt to look both across and behind the available statistics on women in education, in one particular place and time, in order to raise more general questions about women's experiences at the edge of change. As the following discussion shows, there are still several relatively unexplored areas badly in need of further research. This research may be crucial in providing new perspectives on women's future roles in schools, given the temper of the times.

## CONTEMPORARY EDUCATIONAL REFORMS IN CANADA—
## THE GENERAL CONTEXT

Levin (1998) provides an overview of common themes in current school reform initiatives in several English-speaking countries. The need for reform is justified in these countries by calls for a better-prepared, globally competitive workforce. There is large-scale criticism of schools, especially by the corporate sector. The required changes are largely in governance, which is being decentralized, and in the assessment of learning, which is being standardized, and thus centralized. There is considerable emphasis on "choice," that is, greater freedom for parents to choose the schools their children will attend. These choices are made in a market environment where funding is linked to enrollments. Unlike reforms in public education in previous eras, there is now no substantial infusion of government funding to assist in implementation.

Levin and Young (1998) claim that the differences in the school reform initiatives from country to country are as important as the similarities. They note that national contexts differ, and that "local history and practice are [also] powerful influences" (9). Funding is an important example. In some countries, governments have provided limited additional funding during the period when the schools are being expected to implement major changes. In other countries (such as Canada), there have been cuts in both the current and real dollars directed to public schools, despite the expectation that major changes will be implemented. These cuts to public education often are part of more general cutbacks in government spending on human services. The immediate effect on teachers includes reductions in overall staffing, combined with salary rollbacks. Some of the longer-term effects of these cutbacks, particularly on women, are under investigation in this chapter.

## "DEKLEINING" ALBERTA—SPECIFIC HISTORICAL CONTEXT

For two expansionary decades, from the time that oil was discovered in the late 1940s, Alberta outspent other Canadian provinces in its funding for education and other social services (Harrison 1999). But this largesse was closely linked to the government's income from oil and natural gas royalties and to rapid population growth. By the early 1970s, the Alberta government began to reduce the proportion of the provincial budget that was allocated to public schooling (Mazurek 1999). This shift was a consequence, in part, of the Conservative Party's defeat of the Social Credit Party, but it also was a response to declining oil prices throughout the world.

According to Neu's (1999) analysis, while per-student funding in Alberta has increased slightly in constant dollars since 1981, Alberta's expenditure per student had dropped below the national average by the period 1993–1994. Not only is there historical precedent for the recent funding cuts in Alberta, but Mazurek (1999) argues that a (Tory) government-sponsored report released in 1977—the Harder Report—is the "blueprint for changes to education that have taken two decades to fully realize" (14). These changes include, among other things, an emphasis on employment-related training and more time for core curriculum with fewer options and standardized testing.

There also have been numerous mandatory changes in governance, school management, and fiscal structures (Peters 1999). Many of Alberta's publicly funded school districts have been merged into larger jurisdictions (Evans 1999). The province has placed severe legislative restrictions on the size of the "administration" funding envelope available to district central offices. Evans (1999) reports that district responses to the limited administration envelope

have included downsizing the central administration and contracting out services. Other responses have involved shifting the costs for support services
down to the schools.

Concurrently, many management responsibilities have been devolved to
local school sites (school-based management), with a mandated parent advisory council. Many school councils have made fund-raising a major focus.
However, the capacity to raise funds is not equal across schools and districts
(Evans 1999). Meanwhile, as Evans notes, both schools and school boards are
now required to prepare three-year business plans and annual results reports
that include some measure of (parent, teacher, student, community) satisfaction
with the school's/district's efforts.

The budgeting tasks associated with school-based management (SBM)
also are new to most school-site administrators. Commenting on the radically
changed role of the school principal, Yanitski and Pysyk (1999) state that imple-
menting SBM was the "second biggest challenge" after the even greater burden of struggling to accept and implement the funding cuts themselves.

For many individuals, underlying all of these structural adjustments is a
concern about ethical issues. As Evans puts it, "The strategies that enable school
boards to achieve the greatest success in meeting the government's expectations
also have the greatest potential to increase inequities in the educational opportunities for students" (1999, 151). Like many other scholars studying school
reform initiatives (see, e.g., Levin 1998; Peters 1999), she questions the potential of these changes to effect improvements in student learning. In this turbu-
lent and testing environment, where do we find women educators?

## DESPERATELY SEEKING STATISTICS

It is both difficult and important to obtain and maintain statistical data on educators by sex (Young 1995; Gaskell and McLaren 1991). However, the collection of such data has largely been taken for granted in Canada, and perhaps in
other countries, over the past decade. Recently in Canada, both provincial and
federal levels of government have been taking less and less responsibility for
collecting and reporting such information. Indeed, one of the first actions of
Ontario's premier, Mike Harris, was to abolish the provincial law requiring the
collection of equity-related information (Young and Ansara 1999). Meanwhile,
in Alberta, the number of staff in the department overseeing elementary and
secondary schooling has been reduced (Peters 1999), and obtaining pertinent
data is now much more easily said than done.

In 1997, *Education in Alberta: Basic Statistics*, an annual brochure, ceased
publication because of insufficient government staff to prepare it. In that same
year, I obtained funding for a questionnaire survey about part-time teaching
arrangements across the province. Because school districts were still merging
and administrators were still changing posts, my research assistant called every

district to ensure that we used an up-to-date mailing list. We were often referred to a secretary who had been delegated the work of doing manual counts of gender breakdowns from personnel entries on payroll lists. In one instance, a district sent us a printout that listed all teachers by payroll number, with a male/female code, and invited us to do the count ourselves. On another occasion, an administrator phoned to complain about the request for gender breakdowns, asking rhetorically, "Who keeps records according to gender, anyway?" Fortunately I was able to reply that about half of the districts in the province had indeed responded with male/female breakdowns of their teaching staff, in a number of employment categories. Despite both ideological objections and practical difficulties with administrative systems in transition, forty-eight districts—a 74 percent response rate—provided at least some of the information we requested.

The Gender Equity in Education Committee of the Alberta Teachers' Association surveyed Alberta school districts in 1989 and again in 1992 regarding male/female participation rates in a variety of formal roles beyond classroom teaching. The survey also inquired about district policies and practices related to gender and employment equity. But there had been many changes since 1992. Given the changed fiscal structures, the funding cutbacks, and the mandatory merger of school districts, there had been substantial cutbacks to district office personnel—both professional and support staff. Anecdotal information abounded about who "survived" these cutbacks and who was sent out to pasture or back into the field. In response to my concern that so little up-to-date information was publicly available, the committee agreed to repeat its survey during the 1996–97 school year. The response rate was a surprisingly high 92 percent. This compares favorably to the much lower rate of 64 percent in 1992 and 79 percent in 1989. According to Neu (1999) per-student funding in Alberta peaked in 1987, using constant-dollar calculations, and in 1994, using current-dollar figures. Thus the fiscal context for the first two surveys reflects a period of much more generous funding for public education. The most recent iteration of the survey provided information about a time after most of the cutbacks and restructuring had been implemented. Longitudinal data from these three surveys (see Young and Ansara 1999) indicate the two patterns discussed in the next section of this chapter.

## WHERE ARE THE WOMEN EDUCATORS?

Canadian women educators have consistently been underrepresented in all types of administrative roles, despite their high proportions in the teaching workforce ( Nixon and Gue 1975; Rees 1990; Reynolds 1989; Reynolds and Young 1995; Young 1990, 1994). Based on her cross-Canada survey, Rees (1990) reported that women's rate of participation at the level of chief executive officer ranged from 0 percent to 6 percent across the provinces. Slightly more recent U.S. studies (cited in Grogan 1996; Tallerico 1999) have placed women's rate of participation in the superintendency at about 7 percent in the early 1990s.

## DECLINING PARTICIPATION IN "SECOND-TIER" SUPERINTENDENCY

The longitudinal data for Alberta, described in the previous section of this chapter, indicate that during the period of severe cutbacks and restructuring in the 1990s, there has been a sharp decline in women's participation at the second-tier superintendent level (Young and Ansara 1999). This decline contrasts with what Rees (1990) reported as a Canadian trend toward women's earlier increased participation at that level. Increasing numbers of Alberta women in superintendency positions appeared during a brief period in the early 1990s at a time when per-student funding grants were high (Neu 1999). By 1994, Alberta's fiscal and governance restructuring plans were being implemented, and per-student funding had fallen well below the national average (ibid.). That year, the total number of superintendents in Alberta dropped, and the number of women in those positions fell, but their participation rate was comparable to what Rees and Padua (1993) found for Ontario. By 1997, apparently several new superintendent's positions had been created in Alberta, but men were appointed to these positions (Alberta Education 1991, 1995).

The Alberta statistics indicate that the period of cutbacks and restructuring has had particularly negative effects on women's participation in second-tier superintendency roles. The declining number and the proportion of women holding these appointments means that, according to district-by-district data from the most recent Alberta Teachers' Association (ATA) survey, no women are holding appointments at the level of superintendent in two-thirds of Alberta's (sixty-five) school districts (Young and Ansara 1999).

The reduced number of women with the superintendent title has major implications for women's future participation at the level of CEO. There is a reduced pool of female candidates with appropriate experience. For example, based on the ATA data for 1996–1997, there was a pool of four men for every one woman with sufficient experience to become a CEO.

Grogan's (1996) study in one U.S. state suggests that employing districts and aspirants still regard the assistant superintendency as the most "credible" on-the-job preparation for the superintendency. The next best is a high school principalship. Grogan notes that, for women candidates, the presumed "absence" (62) of particular sorts of experience rather than the presence of different experiences is still an issue. Whether the absence of a particular sort of title will be equated to the absence of credible experience is now an open question in Alberta.

There are other questions that are grounded in an extensive scholarly literature related to women's limited participation in leadership roles. To what extent did the boys' club prevail when district mergers steepened the province-wide hierarchy by reducing the number of senior positions that were available? Was seniority the reason for the disproportionate decrease in women's appointments, that is, were "last-in" female associate and assistant superintendents the "first out" when some senior central office positions were eliminated? After assessing their prospects, did some women choose not to apply? Was geographic mobility an obstacle for some women when certain district offices were merged with others that were some distance away?

Some observers will argue that, in Alberta, superintendency-level jobs are not nearly as desirable these days as they once were because of the various sociopolitical and legislative changes that have occurred (Young and Ansara 1999). They will add that very few women (and perhaps fewer men than in the past) are seeking out these appointments. However, it is not clear to what degree women's personal preferences account for their limited participation, and to what degree ever-evolving internal and extra-organizational "rules of control" (Reynolds 1995), related to expectations and opportunities, operate to limit women's participation in roles such as the superintendency.

Alberta has been described as a province with highly individualistic sociohistorical traditions (Denis 1995). According to the responses to the ATA surveys, very few formal gender equity policies exist in Alberta school districts (Young and Ansara 1999). However, for a brief period in the early 1990s, it looked almost "normal" for women to hold quite senior positions—with matching titles—in district central offices. But there was never anything resembling a critical mass (Kanter 1977) of women at that level across the province.

It is likely that the few women in the superintendency in Alberta experienced an extraordinary need for acceptance and inclusion in that elite group (Ortiz and Marshall 1995). Seeing the number of women who had membership in the group shrink might reinforce the importance of fitting in. This reaction might be exacerbated by geographic isolation when the few women are dispersed over large areas, as they are in Alberta. As Chase (1995) demonstrates, for women in these situations, there is little "possibility of developing activist discourse" (194).

INCREASING PARTICIPATION IN THE ELEMENTARY PRINCIPALSHIP

Women's participation in school-site administrative positions has increased across Canada (Cusson 1990). Participation rates in school-site administration, however, vary widely by province (Canadian Teachers' Federation 1999; Cusson 1990). In addition to constituting an increasing proportion of Alberta's overall teaching force, increasing numbers of Alberta's women educators are participating as principals and assistants, or vice principals, in elementary schools. In 1985–1986, 15 percent of principals and assistant/vice principals were women, as were 57 percent of all teachers. Statistics Canada (1998) data show that, by

1995–1996, 31 percent of principals and assistant/vice principals were women, but so were 65 percent of all teachers.

As indicated by Reynolds in chapter 2, women's participation in the principalship varies by position and size of the school. Across Canada, women currently hold only 1 out of every 5 secondary school principalships and 3 out of 10 assistant/vice principalships (Canadian Teachers' Federation 1999). Cusson noted that in 1985–1986, women were almost twice as likely to be administrators in very small elementary schools (fewer than 100 students) than in larger elementary schools.

Only 12 percent of all Alberta principals and 21 percent of assistant principals were women in 1980, and ten years later, there was little change, in that 18 percent of principals and 28 percent of assistant/vice principals were women (Alberta Education 1991). The ATA survey data distinguish between elementary, junior high, and senior high appointments and mirror the national trend of women's concentrated participation in elementary school administration.

According to the ATA data (Young and Ansara 1999), in 1988–1989, women comprised 25 percent of the 642 elementary school principals compared to a rate of 17 percent for Ontario at about the same time (Rees 1990). By 1996–1997 in Alberta, women held 43.5 percent of the 664 principalship appointments in elementary schools. This was two and one-half times the proportion of women principals in junior or senior high schools. Also in 1996–1997, women held 60.6 percent of the assistant/vice principalships in elementary schools, an increase from 40.3 percent in 1988–1989. This is the only type of administrative appointment for which women were in the majority.

Thus while there has been a severe drop in the number of women at superintendent levels, there have been concurrent increases in the numbers of women serving as school-site administrators. But given the Alberta context that I have described, it would be naive to think that this is the whole story. If, some would argue, central office superintendency-level appointments are less desirable than they used to be, that point may just as readily be applied to principalships (Young and Ansara 1999). In spite of the rhetoric about the centrality of the school site, the combined effects of restructuring initiatives and cutbacks have devolved more accountability and politics—but very little discretionary funding or power—to school sites. Thus while more women are taking on jobs as principals and vice principals, it is at a time when those jobs are being redefined (Blackmore 1996, 1999), and the work itself is being intensified and made increasingly complex (Holdaway, Thomas, and Ward 1998; Yanitski and Pysyk 1999; Young and Grieve 1996; Young 1999). This is especially true of the elementary school principalship, a job with little release time or administrative stipend (Acker 1995–1996; Cusson 1990).

Is the principalship becoming a new region of *un*contested territory for women in education? Recent research in Alberta suggests that some principalships are becoming unattractive, and some incumbent principals are giving up their roles and returning to the classroom (Fraser, in progress;Yanitski and Pysyk 1999). Superintendents who participated in a study regarding the selection of principals told researchers: "Many teachers with the potential to be effective principals were discouraged from taking administrative training and/or apply-ing for principalships because they perceived that the position of principal had become less desirable than it was formerly" (Holdaway, Thomas, and Ward 1998, 8). Research focusing on women principals in Britain, New Zealand, and Australia, where restructuring has been in effect much longer than in Alberta, suggests that we may be experiencing a period of transition. The transition affords new opportunities to those women who are ideologically "in tune with the times" (Hall 1996). Meanwhile, however, other women (and men) leave in frustration over—or are defeated by—changing ground rules (Blackmore 1996). The issue of why people leave administrative posts is examined further in chapter 5 of this book. In chapter 6, Strachan describes women leaders who find ways to try to fight for schools that are congruent with their convictions. Some women educators, however, follow another route for their careers, a route that shows up as the second major trend in the Alberta statistics we have examined. They teach on a part-time basis.

## INCREASING NUMBERS OF WOMEN IN PART-TIME TEACHING

In teaching, as in many other occupations, the number of Canadians who are employed part time has increased substantially since the early 1980s (Canadian Teachers' Federation 1996; Krahn 1995; Schellenberg 1997; Statistics Canada 1994, 1998).The general trend away from "standard" jobs—that is, employment by one employer involving full-time work with an expectation of being employed indefinitely—has been widely examined and debated (see, e.g., Betcherman et al. 1994; Negrey 1994). So has the movement toward various forms of "nonstandard" employment, such as job sharing and part-time and temporary contracts (see, e.g., Duffy and Pupo 1992; Krahn 1995; Negrey 1994; Schellenberg and Clark 1996). Although the overall restructuring of employment has been widely discussed from many different perspectives, little systematic scholarly attention has been directed toward this phenomenon as it pertains to Canadian teachers.

Statistics Canada reports (1994, 1998) reveal that the number of part-time educators in Canadian public schools has increased by 60 percent since 1989. That year, about 27,000 (9.3%) of all Canadian public school teachers were employed on a part-time basis.This proportion increased gradually to 10.8 per-cent in 1993, to 12.9 percent—nearly 41,000 teachers—in 1994, and then to 13.7 percent (43,600 teachers) across Canada in 1996. The ratio of part timers to full timers shifted from 1 in 10 (1989) to 1 in 6 (1996).These proportions are national averages, and they do vary from province to province, but the number of teachers employed part time has been growing in most Canadian provinces.

Reflecting this general employment trend, the number of part-time teachers in Alberta increased by 40 percent from 1989 to 1996, while the number of full-time teachers peaked in 1991–1992 and has been decreasing since then (Statistics Canada 1994, 1998). The ratio of Alberta's part-time to full-time teachers changed from 1 in 10 to 1 in 7 (in comparison, the ratio in Ontario shifted from 1 in 11 to 1 in 7). In 1989, about 2,500 (9.5%) Alberta teachers were employed on a part-time basis. This proportion has increased gradually, but steadily. By 1996, the 3,500 part timers comprised 12.6 percent of Alberta's 27,700 teachers. The proportion of part timers in Ontario has changed from 8.3 percent in 1989 to 13.1 percent over the same period.

From 1989 to 1996, over 90 percent of Alberta's part timers were women (Alberta Education 1996).[2] In a 1997 survey[3] of all Alberta school districts (Young et al. 1998), 91 percent of the teachers reported to be on part-time continuing contracts were female. In addition, 81 percent of the individuals reported to be on part-time, term-specific contracts were female. These term-specific contracts might or might not be renewed at the discretion of the employing district.

When discussing the issue of part-time employment, many people today talk about the need for a flexible workforce or, perhaps, a flexible workplace (Duffy and Pupo 1992; Kanter 1977; Negrey 1994; Young 1999). There are important differences between these terms. A flexible work*force* reflects an employer's efforts to increase staffing flexibility and lower its fixed staffing costs through the use of part-time and/or term-certain employment arrangements. This often is an organizational response to the pressures of financial restraint and escalating competitiveness. A flexible work*place*, on the other hand, reflects an employer's efforts to offer a range of optional employment alternatives to standard full-time employment. This is offered in order to give individual employees more flexibility, to tailor their paid work arrangements, and to complement other dimensions of their lives. Both approaches exist in Alberta school districts, often within the same district (Young and Grieve 1996).

Whether a school district strives for a flexible workplace or a flexible workforce, it is influenced by the interaction between Alberta school legislation, its jurisdiction's collective agreement with its teachers, and the district's own administrative policies. Unlike other provinces, Alberta's school legislation includes a provision that gives employing school districts and their administrators considerable freedom to "vary the amount of time that the [part-time] teacher is required to teach, from semester to semester, and from one school year to the next" (School Act 1994, Section 84). Moreover, part-time teachers, employed under Section 84, have no legislative or negotiated rights to move from part-time to full-time status, whatever their seniority, even when full-time teaching contracts are being offered. School boards have, thus far, been unwilling to bargain away the administrative freedoms granted under Section 84.

Our research indicates that the increased use of part-time teaching employment reflects both organizational and individual responses to the legislative and fiscal environment of the 1990s. Both central office and school administrators have stated that their reluctance to forego the flexibility afforded by Section 84 has been exacerbated by the provincially mandated move to school-based management (including budgeting) in combination with the cutbacks. But there are also instances of districts that, as part of their response to severe funding cutbacks, have made new flexible workplace options available to staff who already hold full-time, continuing contracts.

Over one-third of the districts responding to our survey indicated that teachers with regular, full-time contracts may now shift to part-time employment for an agreed-upon period while retaining their full-time, continuing contracts. Each of the part-time agreements is negotiated individually, usually between one teacher and one principal. This type of response promotes flexible work*places* for some fortunate individuals rather than focusing exclusively on flexible work*forces* (Young et al. 1998).

Indeed, our interviews in various districts suggest that where such flexible workplace options are available, teachers on full-time, continuing contracts are using voluntary, part-time arrangements to buy additional preparation time and to alleviate some of the stress related to job intensification (Young and Grieve 1996; see also Saskatchewan Teachers' Federation 1997). Administrators then hire lower-paid new teachers on part-time contracts to fill their staffing needs (see also Blackmore 1999). This obvious cost-saving measure for schools leads to an overall increase in part-time teaching and can be seen to exacerbate a division within teaching between what Kenway and Langmead in chapter 7 discuss as "core" and "casual" educational workers.

It should be noted that part-time teaching is a pattern that reflects the "choices" (Saskatchewan Teachers' Federation 1997, 5) made by individual women as a way of accommodating their domestic responsibilities while remaining in the paid workforce. In the past, most women had no "flexible workplace" option, and women gave up their continuing, full-time contracts to meet their domestic responsibilities to children or aging parents. Such women are now part of the Section 84 group of "flexible workforce" part timers (Young and Grieve 1996). In spite of a difference in their initial motivation— and this does compensate to some extent for their part-time status—these women are just as much affected by changes in policy and practice concerning part-time employment as are other part timers.

Whatever the motive or the positive and negative outcomes of the decisions by individual teachers, our research has revealed an array of micro-politics and moral issues (see, e.g., Young 1999; Young and Grieve 1996), many of which are related to gender (see chapter 2 by Reynolds for a discussion of historical connections between these factors). In our data, several negative school-level effects of staffing with part timers are evident. Both teachers and administrators have told us about highly politicized staffing negotiations between principals and teachers in the name of program needs. Teachers and administrators claim that these negotiations contribute to job intensification and complexification in relation to teachers' work and the work of the principal. Some principals have expressed frustration concerning their inability to support promising new professionals through permanent employment contracts (see also Blackmore 1999; Robertson 1996). Everyone interviewed spoke about uncertainty as a way of life in today's schools (Hargreaves 1994). Teachers' assignments—especially those of part timers—are very dependent on school enrollments and "client" demands for specific courses and programs. Kenway and Langmead also pick up this point in chapter 7 and discuss it in relation to universities. Teachers and administrators across all levels of education in many countries today are struggling to manage, coexist with, or minimize uncertainty in their day-to-day professional life.

Because such a high proportion of the part-time teachers is women, this form of employment is indeed "women's work," and policies and practices related to part-time teaching have differential effects on women's and men's careers and lives. According to our survey (Young et al. 1998), 88 percent of those teachers who make the optional, "flexible workplace," part-time arrangements are female. It remains largely women who avail themselves of the "choice" to work part time as teachers. Do these numbers signal the potential "casualization" (Blackmore 1999; Robertson 1996) of employment for teachers—that teachers are being treated as a flexible workforce to be expanded and contracted, according to employers' needs (Young 1999)? Or, more optimistically, are we seeing the advent in Alberta of schools as flexible workplaces that offer a variety of alternative but equitable employment options for teachers? Whatever one's view of the current situation, the information presented in this chapter suggests a number of questions for further research.

## AREAS IN NEED OF FURTHER RESEARCH

The combination of severe financial cutbacks and restructuring of the governance and administration of public schooling in Alberta has given rise to radically altered structures of opportunity (Kanter 1977) for female and male educators. In Alberta, the statistics quoted in this chapter show that, while women's participation in the superintendency continues to decline, their proportion in the elementary principal and/or vice principal role has increased, as has their participation in part-time teaching posts. All of these observations raise questions about largely unacknowledged differences by gender, in terms of career routes in the teaching profession. When statistics by sex are hard to obtain, as I have illustrated here, it is very difficult to see trends by gender, let alone try to consider how or why they have been constructed and are maintained. Researchers and school practitioners need to ask pertinent questions about gender and school leadership, if we are to affect future trends. The evidence presented in this chapter suggests three areas for further work.

First, we need to know more about the "contested" and "uncontested" roles within schools in particular settings today (Young and Ansara 1999). Drawing on what we know about the past, we need to ask whether current gender and power relations in schools mean that women have given over some roles to men, and whether men have given over other roles to women. In other words, are we seeing stereotypical regendering of roles in schools? Is the superintendent's role in question, or the school principal's? If so, what are the consequences for individuals in each gender group, and for the gender group as a whole, of contestation or noncontestation around such roles? What are the consequences for the overall school system and for society? If roles are being regendered in nonstereotypical or new ways, we also need to consider the implications. It is important for such work to avoid an uncritical reliance on liberalism's edict for viewing career decisions as totally free "choices" made by autonomous, unconnected individual men and women. Rather, we need to think of opportunities within school career routes as social constructions that are very much related to conceptions of gender and other factors, and that are intricately linked to the economic and political context of the times.

A second area that invites further inquiry is how the growth in private or independent schools in various countries may affect male and female teachers' career routes as teachers and administrators. Are debates about single-sex schools arising again? How would the outcome of such debates affect men and women who teach or who wish to take up administrative roles in schools at different levels? While data used in this chapter have focused on Canada's publicly supported schools, many of the questions raised here are important for consideration within the privately funded schools that exist around the globe.

Third, this chapter has discussed trends toward flexible workforces and flexible workplaces in relation to teachers. There is much here that could be explored further. We know little about the impact, if any, of part-time teaching on students or on student outcomes. We also know little about how such work arrangements affect individual men and women, in positive or negative ways. There also is little knowledge about the impact on families or other areas of society when so many women teachers work on a part-time basis. Before we can make judgments about the desirability of the sorts of "nonstandard" employment practices, which schools in Alberta have been shown to be undertaking today, or recommendations about policy and practice, we need more data.

Many of the areas considered here are not entirely new. They have, however, taken on new spins given the era of restructuring in education, which many of us are experiencing at the present time. For that reason, I suggest that the questions I have posed are "new again" and are central to improving the experiences and opportunities of all those who work at the edge of change in schools today.

## NOTES

1. According to Harrison (1999), this term was first used by the provincial government treasurer in his 1995 budget, as justification for the combination of budget cuts and lower taxes.

2. Aggregated data provided by Alberta Education, based on teachers' self-reported information and drawn from annual surveys of all teachers employed in the province for the school years 1989–90 to 1995–96.

3. This survey was conducted as part of my ongoing, multiyear program of research exploring the phenomenon of part-time teaching in Alberta. The research also includes extensive interviews with part-time teachers, full-time teachers, administrators, teachers' association officials, and parents in four Alberta school districts.

## REFERENCES

Acker, S. 1995–1996. "Gender and Teachers' Work." Pp. 99–162 in *Review of Research in Education, vol. 21*, ed. M. Apple. Washington, D.C.: AERA.

Alberta Education. 1991. *Education in Alberta: Basic Statistics, 1991*. Edmonton, AB: Policy and Planning Branch, Alberta Education.

Alberta Education. 1995. *Education in Alberta: Basic statistics, 1995*. Edmonton, AB: Policy and Planning Branch, Alberta Education.

Alberta Education 1996. *Selected Teacher Statistics, 1989–90 to 1995–96*. Unpublished statistics supplied on request.

Betcherman, G., K. McMullen, N. Leckie, and C. Caron. 1994. *The Canadian Workplace in Transition*. Kingston, ON: IRC Press.

Blackmore, J. 1996. "Doing 'Emotional Labor' in the Education Market Place: Stories from the Field of Women in Management." *Discourse: Studies in the Cultural Politics of Education* 17:3:337–49.

Blackmore, J. 1999. *Troubling Women: Feminism, Leadership, and Educational Change*. Buckingham and Philadelphia: Open University Press.

Canadian Teachers' Federation. 1996. "Part-Time Teachers More Than Double Since Early Eighties." *Economic Service Notes* (April 1): Ottawa: Canadian Teachers' Federation.

Canadian Teachers' Federation. 1999. "Female Educators Still Underrepresented in School Administration." *Economic Service Notes* (December–January): Canadian Teachers' Federation.

Chase, S. E. 1995. *Ambiguous Empowerment*. Amherst: University of Massachusetts Press.

Cusson, S. 1990. "Women in School Administration." *Canadian Social Trends* 18 (autumn):24–26.

Denis, C. 1995. "The New Normal: Capitalist Discipline in Alberta in the 1990s." Pp. 86–100 in *The Trojan Horse: Alberta and the Future of Canada*, ed. T. Harrison and G. Laxer. Montreal, Quebec: Black Rose Books.

Duffy, A., and N. Pupo. 1992. *Part-Time Paradox: Connecting Gender, Work, and Family.* Toronto: McLelland & Stewart.

Evans, J. 1999. "Board Games: The New (but Old) Times." Pp. 151–64 in *Contested Classrooms: Education, Globalization, and Democracy in Alberta,* ed T.W Harrison and J. L. Kachur. Edmonton: University of Alberta Press and Parkland Institute.

Fraser, C. (In progress.) *Re-valuing Teachers.* Edmonton: University of Alberta.

Gaskell, J., and A. McLaren, eds. 1991. *Women and Education,* 2d ed. Calgary, AB: Detselig.

Grogan, Margaret. 1996. *Voices of Women Aspiring to the Superintendency.* Albany: State University of New York Press.

Hall, V. 1996. *Dancing on the Ceiling.* London: Paul Chapman.

Hargreaves, A. 1994. *Changing Teachers, Changing Times: Teachers' Work and Culture in the Postmodern Age.* New York: Teachers College Press.

Harrison, T. W. 1999. "The 'Alberta Advantage': For Whom?" Pp. 33–44 in *Contested Classrooms: Education, Globalization, and Democracy in Alberta,* ed. T.W. Harrison and J. L. Kachur. Edmonton: University of Alberta Press and Parkland Institute.

Holdaway, E. A., D. W. Thomas, and K. L. Ward. 1998. "Policies and Practices Involved in the Selection of School Principals." *The Canadian Administrator* 37:4:1–11.

Kachur, J. L., and T. W. Harrison. 1999. "Introduction: Public education, Globalization, and Democracy: Whither Alberta?" Pp. xiii–xxxv in *Contested Classrooms: Education, Globalization, and Democracy in Alberta,* ed. T. W. Harrison and J. L. Kachur. Edmonton: University of Alberta Press and Parkland Institute.

Kanter, R. M. 1977. *Men and Women of the Corporation.* New York: Basic Books.

Krahn, H. 1995. Nonstandard Work on the Rise. *Perspectives on Labor and Income* 7:4:35–42.

Levin, B. 1998. "An Epidemic of *Education* Policy: (What) Can we Learn from Each Other?" *Comparative Education* 34:2 (June)· http://www.library.ualberta.ca/library.html//database/elite.html.

Levin, B., and J. Young. 1998. "International Educational Reform: From Proposals to Results." *The Alberta Journal of Educational Research* XLIV:1 (spring): 91–93.

Mazurek, K. 1999. "Passing Fancies: Educational Changes in Alberta." Pp. 3–20 in *Contested Classrooms: Education, Globalization, and Democracy in Alberta,* ed. T. W. Harrison and J. L. Kachur. Edmonton: University of Alberta Press and Parkland Institute.

Negrey, C. 1994. *Gender, Time, and Reduced Work.* Albany: State University of New York Press.

Neu, D. 1999. "Reinvestment Fables: Educational Finances in Alberta." Pp. 75–83 in *Contested Classrooms: Education, Globalization, and Democracy in Alberta,* ed. T. W. Harrison and J. L. Kachur. Edmonton: University of Alberta Press and Parkland Institute.

Nixon, M., and L. R. Gue. 1975. "Women Administrators and Women Teachers: A Comparative Study." *Alberta Journal of Educational Research* 21:196–206.

Ortiz, F. I., and C. Marshall. 1995. "Becoming a School Leader: The Case of Females and Minorities." *People and Education* 3:1:83–110.

Peters, F. 1999. "Deep and Brutal: Funding Cuts to Education in Alberta." Pp. 85–97 in *Contested Classrooms: Education, Globalization, and Democracy in Alberta*, ed. T. W. Harrison and J. L. Kachur. Edmonton: University of Alberta Press and Parkland Institute.

Rees, R. 1990. *Women and Men in Education.* Toronto: Canadian Education Association.

Rees, R., and S. Padua. 1993. *Employment Equity in Ontario School Boards: A Study of the Formal and Informal Mechanisms for the Promotion of Women in Administrative Positions.* Toronto: Unpublished report for the Ontario Ministry of Education and Training.

Reynolds, C. 1989. "Man's World/Woman's World: Women's Roles in Schools." *Women's Education des Femmes* 7:3:29–33.

Reynolds, C. 1995. "In the Right Place at the Right Time: Rules of Control and Woman's Place in Ontario Schools, 1940–1980." *Canadian Journal of Education/Revue Canadienne de l'education* 20:2:129–45.

Reynolds, C., and B. Young, eds. 1995. *Women and Leadership in Canadian Education.* Calgary: Temeron Books.

Robertson, S. L. 1996. "Teachers' Work, Restructuring, and Postfordism: Constructing the New 'Professionalism'." Pp. 28–55 in *Teachers' Professional Lives*, ed. I. F. Goodson and A. Hargreaves. London: Falmer Press.

Saskatchewan Teachers' Federation. 1997. (October). *The Workload and Worklife of Saskatchewan Teachers.* Saskatoon: Saskatchewan Teachers' Federation.

Schellenberg, G. 1997. *The Changing Nature of Part-Time Work.* Ottawa: Center for International Statistics at the Canadian Council on Social Development.

Schellenberg, G., and C. Clark. 1996. *Temporary Employment in Canada: Profiles, Patterns, and Policy Considerations.* Ottawa: Center for International Statistics at the Canadian Council on Social Development.

*School Act.* 1994. Province of Alberta, Canada. Section 84.

Statistics Canada. 1994. *Education in Canada, 1992–93.* Ottawa: Minister of Supply and Services, Cataglogue #81–229.

Statistics Canada. 1998. *Education in Canada, 1997.* Ottawa: Minister of Supply and Services, Cataglogue # 81–229–XPB.

Tallerico, M. 1999. "Women and the Superintendency: What Do We Really Know?" Pp. 29–48 in *Sacred Dreams: Women and the Superintendency*, ed. C. C. Brunner. Albany: State University of New York Press.

Yanitski, N., and D. Pysyk. 1999. "The Principalship at the Crossroads." Pp. 165–75 in *Contested Classrooms: Education, Globalization, and Democracy in Alberta*, ed. T. W. Harrison and J. L. Kachur. Edmonton: University of Alberta Press and Parkland Institute.

Young, B. 1990. "Not There Yet: Women in Educational Administration." Pp. 85–102 in *Canadian Public Education System: Issues and Prospects*, ed. Y. L. Jack Lam. Calgary: Detselig.

Young, B. 1994. "Another Perspective on the Knowledge Base in Canadian Educational Administration." *Canadian Journal of Education/Revue Canadienne de l'education* 19:4:351–67.

Young, B. 1995. "Postscript: Where Do We Go From Here?" Pp. 243–53 in *Women and Leadership in Canadian Education*, ed. C. Reynolds and B. Young. Calgary: Temeron Books.

Young, B. 1999. "Is It Just a Matter of Time? Part-Time Teaching Employment in Alberta." Pp. 139–49 in *Contested Classrooms: Education, Globalization, and Democracy in Alberta*, ed. T. W. Harrison and J. L. Kachur. Edmonton: University of Alberta Press and Parkland Institute.

Young, B., and S. Ansara. 1999. "Women in Educational Administration: Statistics for a Decade." *The ATA Magazine* 79:2 (winter):22–27.

Young, B., H. Gray, C. Alexander, and S. Ansara. 1998. (June). *Part-Time Teaching Employment in Alberta: The Stories That Statistics Can Tell*. Paper presented at the CASWE Institute, Centering on Margins: The Evaded Curriculum, Ottawa.

Young, B., and K. Grieve. 1996. "Changing Employment Practices? Teachers and Principals Discuss Some 'Part-Time' Employment Arrangements for Alberta Teachers." *Canadian Journal of Educational Administration and Policy* 8: 1–14 (http://www.umanitoba.ca/publications/cjeap).

CHAPTER FIVE


# Women Administrators and the Point of Exit: Collision between the Person and the Institution

---

Patricia Schmuck, Sandra Hollingsworth, and Robyn Lock

*United States*


## INTRODUCTION

There are many definitions of feminism. We particularly like the one by Rebecca West: "People call me a feminist, whenever I behave in a way that would differentiate me from a doormat" (in Faludi 1991). We define feminist scholarship on educational leadership as that which: (1) focuses on the condition of females; (2) articulates embedded assumptions about gender in organizational and interpersonal relationships; and (3) provides theory and suggested action aimed at restructuring power relationships.

This chapter picks up each of these threads by focusing on women who have left a leadership role in education, by questioning what their stories of leaving reveal about embedded assumptions, and by suggesting from this information some ways that women can work for positive change. The chapter begins with an examination of the literature on women as educational leaders. Four extensively explored themes are identified. We point to a significant gap in the literature concerning the "point of exit," that is, examinations of the reasons women leave administrative posts in organizations such as schools. Our first question considers why some women leave school leadership positions at the postsecondary level.

In this chapter we focus on data from interviews with four women who left their administrative role in a college or university setting in the past few years in the United States. Their interviews were part of a larger study that investigated women's reasons for leaving elementary, secondary, or postsecondary school administration, either voluntarily or involuntarily. Our focus here is on the particular experiences of four women in the current university climate in America. The stories of these four women do not allow for generalizations regarding the experiences of all women leaders. However, they do provide rich insights into how some women have acted when their attempts to "transform" their institution did not proceed as planned, and instead they found themselves in collision with the institution. The intention here is to learn all we can from each individual case. This is warranted because we can learn a great deal about the general from studying the specific, but we will never know about the specific by studying only the general (Glesne and Peshkin 1992). As Wolcott (1995) suggests, every case is in certain aspects like all other cases, like some other cases, and like no other case. At the very least, the cases examined in this chapter open doors that largely have remained closed.

What can we learn about gendered politics in particular settings by examining women's accounts? This is our second question. In addressing this, we consider how the sharing of the sensitive and sometimes painful experiences of the four women studied here informs our views about leadership. These women's accounts illustrate some of the pros and cons of conformity and/or resistance and the importance of allies, family, and friends. These stories also reveal how difficult it is to enact a social justice agenda within institutions, such as universities at the present time. We conclude the chapter with a list of practical lessons for others who may find themselves in similar situations such as those described by the four women, whose accounts are examined and discussed.

## BACKGROUND OF THE LITERATURE

The literature on women as educational leaders in elementary and secondary schools from several English-speaking countries (Dunlap and Schmuck 1995; Hall 1996; Blackmore and Kenway 1993; Reynolds and Young 1995; Regan and Brooks 1995; Shakeshaft 1989; Strachan 1999) indicates that women's gains in those countries are strongly related to the feminist movement, the introduction of equal opportunity, and affirmative action policies over the last several decades. Deem and Ozga (1997) point out, however, that women in English-speaking countries generally have not been any more successful in attaining senior posts in education, especially in higher education, than in other areas of the labor market.

We know that the total number of female administrators in education in the United States increased from the period 1976 to 1995. In elementary and secondary schools the percentage of women principals rose from 6 percent to 35 percent, and the percentage of women superintendents went from .01 percent to 7 percent (Brunner 1998). In higher education, the percentage of women in senior administrative posts rose from 5 percent to 16 percent over the same time period (Eggins 1997). The literature regarding this growing number of women school leaders in the United States in these two decades has focused on the following four themes:

1. *Describing Why Women Have Been Invisible in School Administration*

   This literature documents and explains why women, both past and present, have not occupied the majority of administrative posts in the public schools sector (Schmuck 1995; Schmuck et al. 1981; Edson 1988; Shakeshaft 1989) and in higher education (Bensimon and Marshall 1997) in the United States.

2. *Giving Advice about School Administration*

   Another body of literature in America has focused on strategies for improving the participation of women administrators (Kalvelage et al. 1982; Regan and Brooks 1995; Schmuck 1995) and for providing advice for women about how to lead once they have obtained a position as an administrator (Brown and Irby 1993).

3. *Describing How Women Lead in Schools*

   A third area of the literature in the United States has documented how women administrators play out their roles (Shakeshaft 1989; Lambert et al. 1995; Dunlap and Schmuck 1995).

4. *Developing Theory about Gender in Organizations*

   A fourth area of the literature in America has been concerned with the development of theory about gender and power in organizations in general and school organizations in particular (Ferguson 1984; Aisenberg and Harrington 1988; Bensimon 1995).

   Our review of the U.S. literature about women and administration, however, reveals that only a few studies have focused on women *leaving* their administrative posts in education. We argue that there are at least three reasons for this absence in the literature. First, the relatively low numbers of women in school administration have made it difficult to find women school leaders for the purpose of research, or to document their experiences of leaving. Second, existing data about exiting administrators have not been gathered with sex as a variable. Although considerable data exist about superintendent turnover rates in the United States (see, e.g., Davis 1998; Tallerico et al. 1993), few of these studies have included sex as a variable. In the Davis (1998) study, superintendents' perceptions of why school principals were removed from their positions were not differentiated by sex. In the study, there was no mention of the superintendents' or principals' sex, although "interpersonal relationships" were identified as playing a key role in dismissal.

We think interpersonal relationships may mean gendered politics, that is, those politics that position most males in more powerful roles than most females in the organization. We suggest that when the variable of sex is included, we may be able to improve our understanding as to why more women superintendents than men in that role leave involuntarily. A third reason for the gap in the literature with regard to studies of women leaving administrative posts in schools may be because of the difficulty in gathering data on such a sensitive topic. Involuntary and perhaps even voluntary leaving may have presented individuals with painful experiences. Such sensitivities present several ethical difficulties for researchers who wish to undertake studies on this topic. Recognizing the gap in the literature and the reasons for its existence, the authors, as feminist leaders who are concerned about improving our understandings of such things as gendered politics in schools as organizations, designed a study to begin to fill the identified gap.

## METHODOLOGY

In our larger interview study, we conducted a series of interviews to investigate the reasons women described for leaving leadership roles in elementary and secondary schools and colleges and universities. It became clear in that study that postsecondary institutions presented particularly problematic environments for women leaders. Feminist scholars of higher education, such as Deem and Ozga (1997), depict the academy as a patriarchal organization that has seldom lived up to its image as a world of disinterest where universal perspectives are allowed to flourish. (Kenway and Langmead discuss this point in some detail in chapter 7.) Adrienne Rich has pointed out that the academy has long had a "male-defined culture," but because most members, whether male or female, are heavily embedded in that culture they have either been unaware of the male-defined nature of the culture or they have not been troubled by it (Rich 1993, 123).

The focus here is on four particular women within our data pool who were from the university sector. These women told us of having tried to challenge the status quo in their respective institutions prior to leaving. Their stories are used here to explore the dynamics of how individual women's transformative visions can collide with other institutional perspectives and lead to a point of exit.

## THE FOUR STORIES OF EXIT

Though each of the four women we interviewed identified differently along a feminist continuum, all held transformative visions for their institutions. All were successfully reaching their goals, but eventually their visions collided with purposes of the larger institution and brought about their exits. The institutional goals for continuance prevailed over the individual goals for change. Our data suggest that women administrators with a transformative agenda, especially those who articulate a feminist or social justice agenda, may come into collision with the larger educational institution. The gendered political relationships in educational organizations create a different dynamic for female administrators than for male administrators. Males who collide with institutional agendas are often given alternatives to withdraw from the collision, such as lateral promotions or early retirements with favorable press releases to save face. Women's exits, especially feminist women, are more likely to be personally and professionally devastating.

In a structured, two-hour interview, each of the four women considered in this chapter talked about her story of exiting her position. Each held a different post, which included a presidency, a deanship, a department chairship, and a program headship. All of the women chosen for discussion here were from different universities and colleges in the United States, and all had been identified by the researchers as having indicated in their stories that they had a "transformative vision" for their institution. It is argued here that this had an impact on their treatment within the organization and contributed to their decision to exit. Pseudonyms have been used to protect confidentiality. Each woman had different reasons for leaving.

President Janely left an urban university to take up a presidency at a university in a different state. While she had planned to retire from her initial post as president, she chose to leave it because she claimed she had "used up all [her] chips" in a battle with the state chancellor. Her decision to leave was voluntary.

When Dean Hood came to a newly formed graduate school of education in a small university in the Midwest, her mission was to build strong alliances with educational practitioners and upgrade the status of contract faculty. She resigned her deanship upon the request of her president, sued the university successfully for breach of contract, and changed careers to become an author. Her decision to exit was involuntary. Dean Hood recalled the last days of her deanship:

> The guys couldn't understand my success. . . . They thought I must have accomplished something by witchcraft. Women as Witches. . . . It was important I be destroyed. Gentlemen help each other with golden handshakes. . . . We need to have back doors so we don't get burned at the stake.

Chair Thomas was elected by the faculty as head of her Education Department in an urban university in the West. She brought a strong social justice agenda and concrete plans to address the university's mission of "diversity." She wanted to work with the several different ethnic minorities in the community. Two years before her appointment as chair was to end, she was "diselected." To avoid a breach-of-contract suit, university officials created another administrative position for her. She subsequently left the university and now works in a private agency. Her decision was a strange mixture of involuntary change followed by voluntary exit. Chair Thomas recalled the meeting where a motion was made to remove her as chair of the promotion and tenure committee, a motion that carried significant meaning about her role as chair:

> I thought: What have I done? Where have I been? It was the worst day of my life. I had started my period, and I didn't know if I had blood on my clothes. I sobbed in my partner's arms at home. I started seeing a counselor. I didn't see how I could have been so wrong about human potential for justice. I began to doubt how I saw the world.

Professor Nippon was a program head who developed a physical education program for sex equity in a faculty of education at a rural university. She left that position when what she described as the resistance of some female colleagues, male administrators, and students became emotionally damaging. She became a member of a faculty of education at another university. Her decision to leave was voluntary.

## THEMES ACROSS THE STORIES

There were complex interactions between personal, institutional, and societal values evident in the stories we collected about what led to a point of exit from a leadership role for each woman. As an organizing device, we have borrowed from Blackmore (1995) and have identified four themes.

- beyond numerical representation,
- stances on inclusion and democracy,
- equity as outcome, and
- forming new alliances.

### BEYOND NUMERICAL REPRESENTATION

One argument for creating institutions that support feminist perspectives has been that this would serve to increase the numbers of women willing to take on leadership roles within such institutions. In recent decades in the United States, women have tended to be relatively well represented numerically in colleges and faculties of education. But a strong female presence in an institution or a unit does not necessarily mean that feminist perspectives or women leaders will be welcomed or encouraged (Schmuck and Schubert 1995). Indeed, we argue in this section that a masculinist culture can prevail, even when there are women leaders and/or a majority of women in a department or other organizational unit.

Within the theme beyond numerical representation, we have clustered our observations about some of the problems women leaders can encounter even though, or sometimes because, they work with other women. One layer of the theme includes how women leaders may choose to become leaders in areas where there are other women but may be disillusioned when they find out that other women do not support their transformative visions. A second layer within this theme is that women leaders may be accepted initially by their institution and even welcomed as a "savior," only to be denigrated later as they enact their visions for change.

The following quote illustrates how one of our feminist leaders saw a strong representation of women in an organization as a reason to take on a leadership role:

> It was a dream. You couldn't imagine a better place . . . there was a predominantly female faculty and staff, perceptive, innovative teaching, and 90 percent of the students were women. I identified with them—mid-life, underemployed, unrecognized, and bright. (Dean Hood)

Chair Thomas made similar types of remarks about her initial observations about her institution. She noted that women held the positions of provost, vice president for academic affairs, dean of the School of Education and associate dean of the School of Education. In addition, most of the faculty in her department were women. Chair Thomas anticipated a great deal of support for her feminist perspective on leadership due to this strong female presence. This was not the case. In her situation, none of the female administrators identified with feminist perspectives, and only two of the twenty-three women on the faculty were self-identified feminists. Chair Thomas felt that women without feminist perspectives not only failed to support the changes she wanted to accomplish, they actually hindered them.

Professor Nippon echoed these sentiments and claimed that a female colleague had discredited her work on the basis that she had used feminist pedagogy. These are her words about an incident involving one of her female colleagues who complained to the administration:

> She wrote a letter to them indicating that my teaching was substandard because it was feminist. She indicated that feminist pedagogy had no place in physical education classes. She hoped I would be reprimanded.

These observations within our data lead us to conclude that although the rhetoric in most colleges of education proclaims equity and diversity as organizational goals, the culture of Dean Hood's and Chair Thomas' universities was still situated in institutions designed by men for men. It was a masculinist culture based on patriarchy. This masculinist culture was picked up by both women and men in the institution.

Women, in our study, are not the only ones who have made claims about the university as a masculinist culture. Other women also have revealed that they experienced attitudes and behaviors from both male and female colleagues that were disconcerting. In her study of women in higher education, Andrea Spurling (1990) found that women managers claimed that female colleagues often undermined the personal and collective energy of women leaders by focusing on why the new ideas of such women leaders would not work. Women in the organization often tended to be naysayers who impeded new ideas rather than helped women leaders implement improvements. Spurling claimed that such women had become socialized into a masculine form of academic politics. She stated: "They appeared to be locked into academic-type displays of individual intellectual machismo: My argument is stronger than yours" (Spurling 1990, 47).

In many university settings in the United States, studies such as ours and Spurling's (1990), suggest that most men are perceived as being better able to fit into the academic system as presently organized. The "fit" in academe for most women depends on their willingness and ability to adopt the norms of the academy and become more like men. In today's context, that can mean that men and women who thrive in their institutions are more often committed to the norms of competitiveness and behind-the-scenes negotiation rather than openness, democratic relationships, and inclusion. Across historical periods, however, women often have had to give way to dominant images of how they should behave as leaders in education and in other fields. This point is made strongly by Mary Kinnear (1995) in her book *In Subordination: Professional Women 1870–1970* for women in Canada across a number of professions. Further, there is substantial evidence to suggest that "as women proceed in management positions, they may undergo a socialization process whereby they become more like men. In this way, they are able to receive favorable evaluations and to retain their positions" (Middlehurst 1993, 13).

Sometimes women leaders are misread as "one of the boys" when they are recruited. This was the case with Dean Hood, who stated that she was begged to join the faculty because the president "saw me as the most recent savior." When she set out to realize her transformative vision, however, she came under attack. She describes it this way:

> The President just sat back and watched. I was under fire; the jackals attacked the new dog. . . . He always has 2–3 people ready to take the fall. He readily sacrifices his Vice Presidents and Deans. . . . The President told the faculty to isolate me. . . . I realized at that meeting that nobody will back me up. Faculty and staff will run for cover.

This quote suggests that women and men who identify with the institutional goals will more likely be successful in the institution compared to women and men who challenge the institutional goals and norms. Correspondingly, women and men with transformative agendas may come into collision with the institution. However, as we argue, the consequences for men are not as severe because of the gendered nature of university politics, a politics that continues to lead women to choose to exit.

For Chair Thomas, it was less a case of having been misread as of never having had support from her dean, even though that dean had been a woman. While receiving the accolades of the faculty upon her hiring, Chair Thomas indicates in the following quote how she was less sanguine about how she was viewed by her female dean:

> I saw an opportunity to be in a leadership role. I could do something for social justice. I came out in the interview as a strong feminist. I had 100 percent support of the faculty. I don't think I was the choice of the Dean. She wanted someone with a more traditional management background.

President Janely's story also indicated a loss of support due to her efforts to enact a transformative agenda for her institution. She was a well-educated administrator with many years of experience who wanted to transform a devalued urban institution to be on a par with the other more prestigious state university institutions in her state. She said her university was "better than they think they are—but could be better . . . but xxx is not accorded a valued role in this state." When she partially accomplished her goal by winning a major battle, she was simultaneously aware that she had "spent her political chips" with the chancellor and the state board. Thus while she was a savior to her own institution, within the larger state system she represented a challenge to the status quo within the institution itself. To protect her personal reputation and advance her career, she voluntarily chose to exit from her university and to relocate to a new university, even though she had hoped to retire at the institution she had left. When asked whether her femaleness made a difference in the battle, she responded:

> I think my being a woman affected how the information was delivered. You never know what would have happened differently, if I were male. You never have confidence enough to forget you are a woman. I thought I could break through that. It seems institutions are more willing to bring in women when the institutions are in trouble. Hard to know which came first. I have opportunities and liabilities as a woman. I am also associated with an institution that is devalued. My mission was to reinterpret the research mission of a major urban university. It got all tangled up between the low status of the institution within the state system of higher education.

## STANCES ON INCLUSIVITY AND DEMOCRACY

The second theme highlights how the stances these four women took regarding inclusivity and democracy contributed to their decisions to exit their leadership role. Blackmore (1995) comments that feminist leaders who advocate building "a new sense of inclusivity and democracy which does not equate consensual politics in educational communities with a privileged position" (53) most often find themselves at odds with societal and organizational expectations. For some women leaders, such as Dean Hood, the stance on inclusivity and democracy was not always constant. Her stance needed to shift for different venues where she carried out different aspects of her leadership role. For example, in the following quote, Dean Hood explains how the roles she had to play with the President's Council varied from her style within her own college:

> I had my Dr. Jeckell, Mr. Hyde behavior. As I crossed the street from the Graduate School to the President's office, I became Mr. Hyde. I came back as Dr. Jeckell. Whenever I had to go across the street, the staff would help me put on my armor. My behavior as Dean and my behavior with the President were so different. I could play hierarchy, cow-tow to the President, engage in fights, be the "blessed one" and not be sacrificed. Then I could go back across the street and take off my armor, be collaborative, be collegial, listen, and decide by consensus.

Deem and Ozga (1997) interviewed women about the risk of challenging organizational privilege. One told them:

> Many women in management want to encourage involvement . . . .but boys want to play their games and don't like it when you draw attention to that. . . . Male management is very unhappy with criticism or critique, and it gets very defensive and sneery. (Deem and Ozga 1997, 35)

Deem and Ozga concluded that women often feel a need to demonstrate competence and "all the characteristics of masculine, rational management in order to counteract inappropriate or hostile assumptions about women managers" (Deem and Ozga 1997, 35). We believe, however, that rather than providing the established process of masculinist organizations, we need more inquiry and awareness about the conservative nature of higher education. Leaders in higher education must provide more challenges to its conserving role in the society. A female manager with a feminist commitment can use her power to empower others and challenge exclusive institutional policies and practices (Deem and Ozga 1997). This was evident in two of the women we have chosen to focus on for this chapter. Dean Hood told us:

> I wanted to write a tenure policy that did not discriminate between academics and practitioners . . . to create a new institution . . . there was nothing I saw as impossible.

Chair Thomas had dreams of "Leading with Heart":

> I loved the faculty position, and I thought leadership would be an extension of that role. I'd be a participant, Lead with Soul, that Deal and Bolman

wrote about, or focus on the spiritual or mystical side that Margaret Wheatley wrote about. I wrote a wonderful letter to the faculty about wanting to be their heart. I was introduced as "someone who could walk on water," and would help heal the tension of twenty years.

When feminist leaders sustain an agenda of inclusion, despite administrative or faculty efforts to block such an agenda, their involuntary exit may mean that they have to leave before privilege is redistributed and social justice is achieved. Chair Thomas, for example, had a long and strong background in civil rights and organized a national women's rights organization. In her interviews she made clear her perspective on working for social justice, and her beliefs were aligned with the stated mission of the department. Her department served students of many racial and ethnic backgrounds. While her actions were in congruence with the rhetoric of the faculty, she soon learned she would have to appease the faculty in power to succeed at her job. She pressed on with her agenda for inclusion and democracy, however, faculty members who had held significant power in the past administration asked the dean for Chair Thomas' resignation. Since Chair Thomas' goals differed significantly from the dean's, despite a rhetoric of inclusion, the dean supported the status quo and not the feminist agenda of Chair Thomas.

## Equity As Outcome

One might think that the concepts of equity and diversity are congruent, however, we see them as competing paradigms and an important third theme that emerged when we focused on the stories of exit of these four women academics. The underlying concept of *equity* rests in action and redistributive social justice for all, whereas the underlying concept of *diversity* is the existence of difference without any necessary commitment to action or social justice (Deem and Ozga 1997, 33). Initiatives for equity, such as the women's movements, civil rights, and affirmative action, have increased the number of women and minorities as managers in higher education. Nonetheless, the concept of equity is severely challenged by concepts of diversity. Standing behind the banner for "equity" requires action and thus garners more risk. Dean Hood discussed a previous position where she was assistant dean in a large research university where the teacher education program was closed despite the university's rhetorical claims of wanting "diversity":

> I watched the crisis at xxx. They closed every program that served women, children, and the aged. The argument was that these programs are the furthest from the scope of the university's purpose. They kept business and educational administration. Snobbery. I watched the devastation in one year of what took twenty years to build.

Chair Thomas reported progress on trying to validate all faculty, junior and senior, and create dynamic learning communities for the working-class, English-speaking Vietnamese, Chinese, and Spanish students. She supported faculty organizing themselves and groups of students into philosophical cohorts with different approaches to curriculum, but behind the scenes, others were trying to return to the former standard of hierarchical structures. They argued that Chair Thomas' ideas were too expensive. This is what she said:

> I argued the cohorts would be self-sustaining. And they were. They flattened the governance system and allowed more faculty to participate in decision making. But behind the scenes others were working against the equity in allowing distinct programs to coexist with similar resources. This idea was a threat to the whole system; it had implications for a real reorganization of the college.

Like Kenway and Langmead in chapter 7 of this book, we see universities moving toward modeling themselves after bureaucratic business organizations, driven by markets with short-term targets, where people are seen as costs or assets rather than as humans. In contrast, transformative universities are thinking long term, value the worth of people, and are driven by ideas of equity and social justice. In such transformative universities, leadership is seen as visionary, communicative, and empowering of faculty (Deem and Ozga 1997). Dean Hood attempted to set up such a culture at her institution:

> What would a real graduate school look like? . . . I decided I wouldn't fire people. I used group processes to build good programs and make money. . . . All programs were growing, doing great. We were too successful. When you create a new institution, new ways of doing things, you create a revolution. . . . They got rid of me and the new organization.

These four women leaders succeeded in promoting equity. None, however, were part of a transformational, organizational culture that might have nurtured them and helped them achieve even more with regard to equity. In Professor Nippon's case, her attempts as a lesbian educator to promote equity in sports and academics in a traditional institution led to personal stress. She lacked support not only from colleagues but from the male students in her secondary teacher education classes. She stated:

> One student, Jason, confronted me in my office. His words were angry and full of hate. He shouted: "Feminism! Feminism! That's all you know. We're sick of it and we're sick of you!" I don't remember breathing, but I must have. He kept up his verbal assault, even as I turned my back on him and walked out. I used the exit leading to the parking lot behind the building where I sat on a parking curb between two cars and cried. My original intention in the class was to examine structures of dominant ideology by giving voice through an examination of power relationships. But the ideological structure of the classroom was used to turn the examination on its head. Continuing discussions of race, class, and gender proved problematic.

Eventually Professor Nippon chose to leave her ranked position in search of a more transformative university culture. Her story, along with President Janely's, shows us that it is important to be committed to action and also to be prepared to change course and take up another project when necessary.

## FORMING NEW ALLIANCES

To transform an organization from individualism and competitiveness to collectivism and cooperation, it is necessary for leaders in top administrative positions, such as President Janely and Dean Hood, to form new alliances while protecting their own positions. Alliances can be built with groups that value social justice. If alliances are not built, the stories from the four women described here suggest that feminist administrators can end up having short career spans. Women administrators who are feminists can have a love-hate relationship with the universities they help lead. Many have "grown up" within the university context. The academy has provided a new life, especially for those feminists from working-class backgrounds. While they may challenge the academy, it also is their lifeblood. After her exit, Dean Hood traveled for a year, visiting friends all over the United States, and found secluded places to write while her suit against the university for wrongful dismissal was being successfully argued. She said:

> Universities have sustained me all my life. I can't imagine I won't have that connection. What do I want to do? What I want is to see people I love. So I did.

All four of these women who exited from their leadership role talked about the difficulty of maintaining personal health and social relations outside of the university with their demanding schedules. They recognized the need for personal relationships, particularly since three of the women had grown children and were divorced or widowed, and two were in a current life relationship.

Dean Hood initially rejected the offer to apply for the deanship because of the recent death of her husband. The overwhelming support she received from the search committee and the president, plus the number of women at the university, caused her to change her mind. Chair Thomas knew her position would be challenging, yet she saw the position as one that would fit her personal values and beliefs and allow her to relocate closer to her children and grandchildren. She said:

> I was ready to leave my current position. I was told how dysfunctional this place was, but I never felt there was a challenge I couldn't handle. I had changed my life so many times; divorce and recognizing I was lesbian, having a father that committed suicide, son dropping out of school. I had faced so many life challenges. So I came.

In the case of Chair Thomas, the stress of the faculty resistance to change led to serious damage to her health. She told us that if she had had a better sense of the balance of her personal and institutional life, she felt she might have accomplished more. She also thought that if she had made better use of alliances with friends and family, she might have voluntarily resigned from her position at an earlier time and thus would have protected her health.

In Rosemary Deem's and Jenny Ozga's interviews with eighteen feminist managers in the United Kingdom, it was troubling to learn that few mentioned their personal lives outside of their jobs. The stories of our four women and the findings by Deem and Ozga suggest that reconnecting with life beyond the job is important to feminist women leaders so they can sustain their demanding agenda toward social justice.

A second form of creating new alliances is to organize networks for support and education. "There is an argument that says that women simply have to learn the rules and that until they do, they will not succeed" (King 1997, 92). Learning such rules, within a formal or an informal women's professional network, is a key feature of sustaining feminist leadership. Networks can help women articulate a language and style that is both individual and allows them to communicate with the existing culture. Hopefully, through discussion, example, and support, groups can help each individual maintain her uniqueness enough to make significant changes where these changes are needed and when each individual reaches a position of leadership.

Helping women get onto the path to the top, stay on it without collapsing from loneliness or isolation, and still maintain their own ways of working is a major role for any successful professional network (King 1997, 98).

There is something special when feminist women come together. Perhaps one of the most compelling and powerful experiences that women have in feminist conferences and workshops for women is the camaraderie, the shared, unspoken assumptions, and the revelation of one's life experience that is understood. It has been proclaimed as overwhelming, a life experience, something "where my toes met my brain in a new way. I was whole" (Schmuck 1995, 216).

In each of the four stories outlined in this chapter, the goals of the exiting administrators were at odds with their institution, although often their goals matched the institutional rhetoric. How can one make the goals of social justice the goals of the institution (Lambert et al. 1995)? It is an incremental process; one must remain true to the vision and be skillful enough to use the power of the position to change the institution. This is a monumental task. Without envisioning a different form of networking, few may be able to accomplish this. President Janely talked about how her perspective had changed from one of "opposing the hegemony of the institution" to "becoming the institution." She remarked:

With the mantle of responsibility I put on now, as President of the institution, I can no longer speak against the institution. I *am* the institution. It is your job—young feminists—to keep challenging me.

## CONCLUSIONS

We are feminist leaders and scholars. Indeed, it was our own passion to change institutions of higher education, including our own, which led us to investigate why women leaders exit from leadership roles in education. We see the need for leaders with courage, experience, insight, and ability to envision a change in the hierarchical and patriarchal culture of higher education. Leaders with such vision clearly stand out from other women and men who see their jobs as the continuance of the status quo of the institution.

Not all women administrators hold transformative visions for their institutions. Women are not of one cloth. Some have a feminist agenda for change, and others share the goals and norms of the larger university and act for its continuance. Some women administrators "play the game" and support those in power in order to further their academic career. Some women administrators may begin with an overt feminist agenda but give it up to survive within the academy. And some women actually encourage the voluntary or involuntary exits of women leaders.

We have argued here that feminist leaders tend to want to create institutions that are democratic and egalitarian. Such leaders want organizations with symmetrical power relations, and they dream of organizations where diverse points of view are authentically represented. We believe that more individuals are needed who hold a feminist agenda and share a commitment in supporting these goals. Unfortunately, as the stories of the women we have focused on in this chapter illustrate, organizations too often do not allow feminist leaders to move through their ranks. Mechanistic structures do not work well for individuals who need an organic structure. This often leads to conflict. Instead of having an opportunity for growth and development, individuals can be encouraged to develop a continuance of the status quo (Louis 1980). In light of all these observations, one of our questions is: How can organizations such as universities and colleges help develop and support feminist leaders?

Feminist leaders are scholars who recognize the need to dismantle systems of power and to achieve equity through personal, political, societal, and institutional transformations. The stories of the four women discussed in this chapter reveal that in some cases collision between the institution and the individual can lead to exit from the organization. What advice do these women give to others who might want to try to do some of the things they tried to do? How do they think others might avoid the collision they encountered? The following list of recommendations comes from the four women focused on in this chapter:

1. Action, not just rhetoric, is required for a feminist agenda.

2. Celebrate small and incremental changes leading to a social justice agenda.

3. Teach your staff and allies how to be leaders for change. Teach and empower others to enact a social justice agenda. Do not do it all yourself.

4. Create alliances inside and outside of the institution that can sustain and assist your efforts for social justice and also help you maintain your good health.

5. Pick your battles carefully. Pick those you have a chance to win. Relish and celebrate when you win but do not worry too much about those you lose.

6. Use the popular media to write and talk about how the universities can lead toward social justice.

7. Remember to connect with family and friends for fun, for joy, and for support.

8. When you enter the institution, consider how you want to leave it. Know when to leave, and consider all of the personal positives that such leaving may entail.

## REFERENCES

Aisenberg, N., and M. Harrington. 1988. *Women of Academe: Outsiders in the Sacred Grove.* Amherst: University of Massachusetts Press.

Bensimon, E. M. 1995. "Total Quality Management in the Academy: A Rebellious Reading." *Harvard Educational Review* 65:4:593–611.

Bensimon, E. M., and C. Marshall. 1997. "Policy Analysis for Postsecondary Education: Feminist and Critical Perspectives." Pp. 1–22 in *Feminist Critical Policy Analysis: A Perspective from Post-Secondary Education*, vol. 2, ed. C. Marshall. London: Falmer Press.

Blackmore, J. 1995. "Breaking Out from a Masculinist Politics of Education." Pp. 44–56 in *Gender and Changing Educational Management*, ed. B. Limerick and B. Lingard. Rydalmere NSW, Australia: Hodder Education.

Blackmore, J., and J. Kenway. 1993. *Gender Matters in Educational Administration and Policy: A Feminist Introduction.* Washington, D.C.: Falmer Press.

Brown, G., and B. Irby. 1993. *Women As School Executives: A Powerful Paradigm.* Huntsville: Texas Council on Women School Executives.

Brunner, C. 1998. *Scattered Dreams: Women and the Superintendency.* Albany: State University of New York Press.

Davis, S. 1998. "Superintendent's Perspectives on the Involuntary Departure of Public School Principals." *Educational Administrative Quarterly* 34:1:58–90.

Deem, R., and J. Ozga. 1997. "Women Managing for Diversity in a Postmodern World." Pp. 25–40 in *Feminist Critical Policy Analysis: A Perspective from Post-Secondary Education*, vol. 2, ed. C. Marshall. London: Falmer Press.

Dunlap, D., and P. Schmuck. 1995. *Women Leading in Education.* Albany: State University of New York Press.

Edson, S. 1988. *Pushing the Limits: The Female Administrative Aspirant.* Albany: State University of New York Press.

Eggins, H. 1997. *Women As Leaders and Managers in Higher Education.* Buckingham: Open University Press.

Faludi, S. 1991. *Backlash: The Undeclared War on Women.* New York: Crown.

Ferguson, K. 1984. *The Feminist Case against Bureaucracy.* Philadelphia: Temple University Press.

Glesne, C., and A. Peshkin. 1992. *Becoming Qualitative Researchers: An Introduction.* New York: Longman.

Hall, V. 1996. *Dancing on the Ceiling.* London: Paul Chapman.

Kalvelage, J., P. Schmuck, and M. Smith. 1982. *Women Getting Together and Getting Ahead.* Newton, Mass.: Educational Development Center.

King, E. Joyce, ed. 1997. *Preparing Teachers for Cultural Diversity.* New York: Teachers College Press.

Kinnear, M. 1995. *In Subordination: Professional Women 1870–1970.* Montreal: McGill-Queens University Press.

Lambert, L. et al. 1995. *The Constructivist Leader.* New York: Teachers College Press.

Louis, M. R. 1980. "A Surprise and Sense Making: What Newcomers Experience in Entering Unfamiliar Organizational Settings." *Administrative Science Quarterly* 25:226–51.

Middlehurst, R. 1993. *Leading Academics.* Buckingham: Open University Press.

Regan, H. B., and G. H. Brooks. 1995. *Out of Women's Experience: Creating Relational Leadership.* Thousand Oaks, Calif.: Corwin Press.

Reynolds, C., and B. Young, eds. 1995. *Women and Leadership in Canadian Education.* Calgary: Temeron Books.

Rich, A. 1993. "Toward a Woman-Centered University." Pp. 121–34 in *Women in Higher Education: A Feminist Perspective,* ed. J. S. Glazer, E. M. Bensimon, and B. K. Townsend. Needham, Mass.: Ginn Press.

Schmuck, P. 1995. "Advocacy and Organizations for Women School Administrators— 1977–1993." Pp. 199–244 in *Women Leading in Education,* ed. D. Dunlap and P. Schmuck. Albany: State University of New York Press.

Schmuck, P., W. W. Charters, Jr., and R. Carlson. 1981. *Educational Policy and Management: Sex Differentials.* New York: Academic Press.

Schmuck, P., and J. Schubert, eds. 1995. "Women Principals' Views on Sex Equity: Exploring Issues of Integration and Information." *Women Leading in Education.* Albany: State University of New York Press.

Shakeshaft, C. 1989. *Women in Educational Administration.* Newbury Park, Calif.: Sage.

Spurling, A. 1990. *Women in Higher Education*. Cambridge: King's College.

Strachan, J. 1999. "Feminist Educational Leadership in a Neo-Liberal New Zealand Context." *Journal of Educational Administration* 37:2:121–38.

Tallerico, M., J. Burstyn, and W. Poole. 1993. *Gender and Politics at Work: Why Women Exit the Superintendency*. Fairfax, Va.: The National Policy Board for Educational Administration.

Wolcott, H. 1995. *The Art of Fieldwork*. Walnut Creek, Calif.: AltaMira Press.

CHAPTER SIX


# FEMINIST EDUCATIONAL LEADERSHIP:
# NOT FOR THE FAINTHEARTED

---

Jane Strachan

*New Zealand*


## INTRODUCTION

Recent New Zealand research (Robertson 1991; Wylie 1994) has shown that neo-liberal educational reforms have made it increasingly difficult for school principals to remain educationally focused in their leadership. School leaders have become more managerial (Codd 1990) and less able to focus on issues of social justice (Codd 1993). They also have had to work increasingly long hours (Keown, McGee, and Oliver 1992; Mitchell et al. 1992; Robertson 1991, 1995; Wylie 1995, 1997). The first question in this chapter asks what all this means for women leaders who have declared themselves "feminists" and who are striving to lead in their schools in feminist ways.

The chapter draws on an in-depth study of the leadership practice of three secondary school principals in New Zealand. Each of these women called herself a feminist, and each claimed that feminism influenced her practice as a school principal. The second question pursued in the chapter is, "What do the three women studied have in common?"

Picking up on one of the themes from the proceeding chapter, that women are often nonsupportive of feminist women leaders in school settings, I argue that we may fall into the trap of being too hard on feminist leaders and expecting too much of them. We need to understand the contextual factors that affect their efforts to lead in feminist ways. As the following discussion shows, there are many types of feminism and many ways to lead in schools according to a feminist agenda. For some feminist leaders, such as the four described in the previous chapter by Schmuck, Hollingsworth, and Lock, the result of attempts at feminist leadership may end up in collision with the institution and result in exit from a leadership role. For other feminist educational leaders, such as the three who are discussed in this chapter, similar attempts result in respect from both staff and parents in the school. There also is a measure of success in terms of having achieved the feminist goals to which the women aspired. The chapter concludes with a discussion of what may account for such differing stories about feminist leadership in school settings.

## THEORETICAL FRAMES

For too long we have expected feminists to be saints or at least to want to achieve sainthood. The fact is, we expect too much. Being a feminist is not like joining an order of nuns. Feminism has to allow itself to encompass the full range of human behavior, from the best to the worst (Mitchell 1997, 47).

Susan Mitchell, for her book *Icons, Saints, and Divas* (1997), interviewed fifteen women whose writing she considered had had a profound impact on the women's movement. They are high-profile women, for example, Gloria Steinem, Betty Friedan, Erica Jong, Alice Walker, and Marilyn French, to name some. In speaking of their work and writing, she comments, "What draws us to them is the work that has emerged from their lives; it is this that transforms and transcends them. Bold, daring, challenging, it captured our minds and hearts" (263).

This transforming work also is being carried out by women who are not internationally high profile, not celebrities. Like the women Susan Mitchell interviewed, they are not perfect, and sometimes their theory is not always matched by their practice. What they do have in common is that they are outspoken, feisty, passionate, and courageous in their fight against oppression and patriarchy.

Feminism offers a number of different theoretical positions that help explain women's experiences in education and educational leadership in particular. So how might liberal, radical, socialist, and poststructuralist feminist perspectives explain the experiences of women educational leaders? It is not my intention here to give a detailed explanation of the different feminisms. Rather, I offer a brief explanation as a backdrop to this chapter.

Liberal feminism is "individualist in orientation" (James and Saville Smith 1992, 33), and liberal feminists believe that women's subordination is due to their socialization. Women are the victims of sex-role stereotyping that limits their potential, and it is this socialization that has prevented them from obtaining their individual rights. Equal Employment Opportunity (EEO) policy and practice is one of the platforms used by liberal feminists to increase women's representation in both senior and nontraditional positions. Reform is the plat-form for improving women's position and takes the form of breaking down barriers and changing attitudes. On the whole, systems are left unchallenged, and strong, hierarchical leadership is privileged (Blackmore 1993).

Given the above, a liberal feminist perspective views women principals as needing to "resocialize," to become more assertive and less passive, more ratio-nal and less emotional, more objective and less intuitive, and more "male" in their exercise of leadership. Change in behavior will happen through education as people realize the detrimental effects of male hegemony on both the indi-vidual and the organization (James and Saville Smith 1992). Blackmore (1989) has been sharply critical of this view, as she believes that it does nothing to redefine leadership to include women's experiences. It continues to give valid-ity to the male norm. Liberal feminists maintain that once women are in orga-nizations in numbers more accurately representative of their representation in the wider world, then this "critical mass" will influence the organization to be more caring and successful.

In contrast to liberal feminism, radical feminism is collective in orienta-tion. Women are viewed as oppressed, and men are seen as the oppressors. Many radical feminists see fundamental differences between men and women. Men are cast as aggressive and violent, and women are scripted as caring and nur-turing. The effect is that men take control and therefore have power (James and Saville Smith 1992). These differences are claimed to stem from the family, where women are vulnerable because of their child-rearing responsibilities. In this view, biology determines relationships within the family, and these rela-tionships are reproduced in all sectors, including schools. There is an unequal sharing of power.

Radical feminists such as Dale Spender believed that within the school system men had established systems and practices for the benefit of men and, because men got there first, they held all of the powerful positions. Men had decided what would be taught on the basis of the limited evidence available to them from their male experience (Spender 1989). For some radical feminists, this explained why women were not principals in representative numbers, given the participation of women at such high rates in the teaching profession in many countries. They argued that "men got there first" (Spender 1989, 39) and set up the systems that ensured their continued access to and control of positions of power. Men ensured that those appointed to principalships were those who perpetuated male control and power.

This meant that women in positions of power worked in systems that were male "friendly," systems that did not value women's ways of leading because the male way was the only valid way. The male "lust for power" (Elshtain 1987, 208) ensured that women practiced their leadership in ways acceptable to men rather than having developed their own unique style (Spender 1989). The oppressive organizations that deliberately excluded

women from the processes of power required "reconstructing or deconstructing the organization's very roots" (James and Saville Smith 1992, 35).
Blackmore (1993) comments that a radical feminist perspective on educational leadership, "does not have any developed theory of how particular processes
and practices are more inclusive, participatory, or democratic but tends to consider power to be purely repressive and possessed by males and located in formal institutions" (5).

Socialist feminism suggests that not all women experienced oppression in
the same way or to the same degree. Some socialist feminists agree with many of
the viewpoints held by liberal and radical feminists, for example, the importance
of equal employment opportunities and the "collective liberation" of women
(James and Saville Smith 1992, 34). However, most socialist feminists are critical
of the fact that neither radical nor liberal feminists have tended to include a class
or an ethnic analysis in their perspectives (Middleton 1993). For example, the
experiences of a white, middle-class principal might be vastly different from those
of a principal from a working-class background, a Maaori woman principal, or a
lesbian. In some cases, women may experience multiple cases of oppression; as a
woman, as a Maaori, as a lesbian, and as a working-class individual.

While agreeing with the radical feminist viewpoint, that organizational
structures and practices can be oppressive to women, although not in themselves anti-women (James and Saville Smith 1992), most socialist feminists view
organizations within the wider context of a social, economic, and political
landscape. Does what happens in the organization influence what goes on in
this wider context, and vice versa? From a socialist feminist perspective, there
may be a tension between the educational and leadership goals of the principal and the "demands" of a market-driven, economic philosophy that requires
quantifiable outcomes.

Labeling feminists and types of feminism can be dangerous. The labels
often make feminist positions appear simplistic. Poststructuralism offered feminism a tool for analysis that highlighted contradictions and shifting positions.
"Subject" and "subjectivity" were central in theory and women's experience.
Subjectivity was "the conscious and unconscious thoughts and emotions of the
individual, her sense of herself, and her ways of understanding her relation to
the world" (Weedon 1987, 32). Weedon said that because women's subjectivity had been historically and socially constructed, the individual was the site for
"conflicting forms of subjectivity" (33). This meant that contradiction was part
of a woman's daily experience (Blackmore 1993). Blackmore explains that the
relevance of feminist poststructuralism to educational leadership theory is that
it acknowledges that women will feel and act differently in various situations.
For example, a woman may lack esteem in some situations but not in others.
Women are not just shaped by social structures, "They actively take up their
own discourses through which they are shaped and by which they shape themselves (Blackmore 1993, 8).

I found Blackmore's statement relevant to me and to the shaping of my study of feminist educational leaders. As I reflected upon my own feminism and its theoretical eclecticism, its shifting nature was apparent. In brief, I believe in equal employment opportunity, affirmative action, and taking personal responsibility. I also believe in collective action, that schools are patriarchal and advantage men over women. I believe that the wider social, economic, and political climate impacts at the school level, and that liberal and radical feminism has tended to be race and class blind. At times I feel strong and am outspoken about social justice issues, and at other times I either choose to be silent or I feel silenced by the attitude or behavior of others. I also feel uncomfortable with the research that focuses on gender and leadership and categorizes men as leading in one way and women in another. In much of that research, differences among men and women are not acknowledged. For this reason, I chose not to impose my own personal view of feminism on the women who participated in this study but to accept that their perception of their feminism was valid. Whether they viewed themselves as liberal, radical, socialist, poststructuralist, or eclectic was not the issue. The issue was whether their understanding of feminism informed their educational leadership practice.

The literature suggests that leadership that is informed by feminism has an altogether different focus than that of neo-liberal managerialism. According to Grundy (1993) certain principles underpin feminist educational leadership practice. These "underpinning philosophies" include emancipatory practice that is committed to working for social justice and equity, contesting and resisting injustices, shared power, and the "emotional" and ethic of care in leadership practice, with a particular emphasis on delivering quality education to students. When selecting the women for this study, each acknowledged that she too subscribed to the principles of feminist leadership articulated by Grundy.

## THE CONTEXT

Over the past ten years the changes in how education is delivered and managed in New Zealand have been massive. I undertook a study that explored how feminist educational leadership was played out in this chaotic, shifting, and complicated context.

The need for improved efficiency and equity permeated the education reforms. The neo-liberal ideology that underpinned the reforms suggests that schools would be more efficient and equitable in their delivery of education if they had to compete for students. Reducing the state's involvement through the devolution of, for example, decision-making and financial responsibilities was another suggested key strategy for improving efficiency and equity. Schools were to be held both financially and educationally accountable through a process of regular monitoring by an external audit agency. A new national curriculum was established that also included regular assessment of students' performance at both the individual and national levels. In brief, schools were required to be more involved in decision making at the local level, to involve their parent community more in the decision-making processes, including the governance of the school, and to be more accountable (Strachan 1999). That was the theory, but what of the reality?

In New Zealand, every school is given a socioeconomic scale decile ranking (SES). These rankings range from 1 (the lowest) to 10 (the highest) and are based on, among other factors, the income of the caregiver population. In a competitive school market, caregivers often enroll their children in those middle-class schools that emphasize strong academic performance as shown by national examination passes and student discipline. With the dezoning of schools, many middle-class caregivers are choosing to bypass their local school, especially if it has a high proportion of ethnic minority students, to send their child to those schools that promote academic performance and student discipline. These schools usually have a low percentage of ethnic minority students. Promoting equity publicly is not given priority. Many of these schools are bursting at the seams and having to control their student intake, often by "creaming off" top students from other schools and refusing entry to "less desirable" students (Watson et al. 1997).

In contrast, many low socioeconomic schools that have high proportions of ethnic minority students, particularly Pacific Islanders and Maaori, are fighting for survival. It is not by promoting equity that schools attract students. Promoting a conservative, middle-class, academic image is more successful (Strachan 1999). Lower socioeconomic schools cannot compete academically with their middle-class counterparts. The backlash from the middle-class community is evidenced when those caregivers who can afford to send their children elsewhere do so (Hawk and Hill 1997). This results then in an obvious tension between needing to provide an equitable, just, and caring education without at the same time alienating caregivers.

Educational leaders, in particular those who are principals of low socioeconomic schools, have been forced to consider and implement creative strategies for resolving this tension. In chapter 1, Valerie Hall suggests that entrepreneurialism could be viewed as a creative form of management that may assist school leaders to work more effectively within a managerialist framework. In New Zealand, there is evidence that feminist leaders also are using entrepreneurial activities to assist them in achieving their equity goals (Strachan 1999).

Having explored the neo-liberal, New Zealand education context, in which the new managerialism is deeply embedded, I now turn to feminism in relation to educational leadership and feminist educational leadership. I do this as an entree to the main course, a study of the leadership practice of three feminist school principals.

## THE STUDY

Feminist educational leadership in context, both micro (the school) and macro (the New Zealand neo-liberal educational climate), was the focus of this study. I explored how three feminist women principals perceived their own feminist leadership, how they played out that role, and what that took in terms of emotional energy, time, and relationships. The neo-liberal context in which these women were operating was one of site-based management. Recent New Zealand research has shown that school principals have found it increasingly difficult to remain educationally focused in their leadership (Robertson 1991, Wylie 1994), have become more managerial (Codd 1990), have been less able to focus on issues of social justice (Codd 1993) and have had to work increasingly long hours (Keown, McGee, and Oliver 1992; Mitchell et al. 1992; Robertson 1991, 1995; Wylie 1995, 1997), with a resultant increase in burnout and stress (Keown et al. 1992).

In 1996, Kate's school had a decile ranking of 5; her student population was 87 percent European, 10 percent Maaori, 2 percent mainly fee-paying Asian students, and 1 percent a mixture of other nationalities. Marie's school had a decile ranking of 4; the student population was 58 percent European, 13 percent Maaori, 20 percent Pacific Islanders, and 9 percent a mixture of other nationalities. Jill's school, with a decile ranking of 2, had students who were 24 percent European, 20 percent Maaori, 30 percent Pacific Islanders, and 26 percent other nationalities, mainly of Asian origin.

Unlike the women in Valerie Hall's study (chapter 1), Kate, Marie, and Jill all viewed themselves as committed feminists whose feminism informed their leadership agenda, yet each was playing out that leadership in very different contexts. Not only were the student populations different, so were the school locations. Kate's school was in a small rural town. Marie's and Jill's schools were both centrally located in a large city.

As I proceeded with my research, which involved multiple interviewing of each of the three women, observation of their leadership, interviewing staff, and the collection of relevant documents, it soon became apparent that even though each defined herself as a feminist leader, each played that out very differently. This difference was largely dependent upon the very different needs of the student populations. However, there was something the women had in common. They were all feisty, forceful, uncompromising, stubborn, and at times difficult to work with. Yet this appeared necessary so that they could stay focused on their feminist agenda. And like the women administrators in Hollingsworth's, Schmuck's, and Lock's (1998) study, described in the preceeding chapter of this book, the women in my study (Strachan 1999) all held "transformative agendas" (4). They sought to "achieve equity through personal, political, societal, and institutional transformations" (3).

The data reveal two major themes. The first is that these women under-took their leadership work with "passion." The second theme is that, perhaps in direct relation to that passionate type of approach to leadership, they gained respect from those in their organization, a respect that I argue was a major fac-tor in their ability to stay in their role and achieve their goals.

## THEME 1—PASSION

What was clear was that each of the women I studied held very strong posi-tions on how best to provide a quality education environment for the students in their schools. "Passionate" and "driven" were words used by others to describe the women's leadership. Their passion and drive helped ensure that the values they held dear were realized in their feminist leadership practice. On the whole, staff also subscribed to the same values as the feminist principals. It would be difficult to object to, for example, the importance of providing a safe learning environment. However, in the next part of this chapter, I illustrate how it was in the implementation of practices that would support highly prioritized aspects of school life (such as the commitment to anti-violence, supporting "at-risk" students, and collaborative and consensual decision making) that working relationship difficulties developed between the principals and other members of the school community.

The women's passionate commitment to their feminist leadership agenda saw them working at the cutting edge of change, a cutting edge sharpened by the neo-liberal managerial context. In their leadership practice, there were many examples of their feistiness. *All* of the women were com-mitted to anti-violence, to supporting "at risk" students, and to collaborative and consensual decision making. However, to illustrate the intense emotion-al quality in their work, I have focused on just one example from each woman's work as a school leader.

### Kate's Work on Anti-Violence

Kate was committed to providing students and staff with a safe learning envi-ronment. She commented, "I will not work where children are walking around with the fear of physical harm." So one of Kate's first and non-negotiable actions was to ensure a safe learning environment that included a "no drugs" policy. Some saw her as uncompromising and inflexible. Being uncompromis-ing and consistent about what she wanted alienated some staff and some pock-ets of the community. It took a great deal of determination and belief in what she was doing to continue to follow the path she chose. Some staff who did not share her vision left. Others were convinced and supported her vision and the path toward it. Yet others were somewhere in between. There was friction with some parents, who were vocal in their opposition of Kate's strong stance on dis-

ciplinary issues. In mid 1996, Kate received a great deal of national media attention. Her school suspended fourteen students for smoking cannabis at school.
The incident was the focus of a number of television programs. Kate's principalship was publicly dissected by the media. Debate raged about whether the
suspensions were justified or not. Parents of the suspended students, lawyers,
other school principals, and social workers were all asked to give their opinion
in the media. Was suspension justified? Should the suspended students be given
another chance? These were two frequently asked questions. Kate and the
school board remained adamant. They believed they were justified, but Kate
was cast as the "witch."

I was not in the least surprised by her actions. It was entirely consistent
with her strong stance on providing a safe learning environment. However,
Kate herself was aware that her inflexibility on some issues made her appear
aloof to others.

> The downside is that some people find me inflexible (and I am on some
> things), some people have found me difficult to get to, and I can't quite
> understand that because I'm always here. Some people have found that I
> am cold and aloof, and I am and always have been . . . when I am looking
> at them [staff] I can see in their eyes this vision of the witch hopping on
> the broom and flying around the school. (Kate)

## JILL'S WORK WITH "AT RISK" STUDENTS

Jill's commitment to working with "at risk" students was overt. With an SES
decile ranking of 2, her school had a high proportion of students with special
needs. Some staff commented that, "She [Jill] has a passionate commitment to
the underdog, to social injustices, [Jill] would not be the principal of a school
with advantaged kids . . . she has a social mission in teaching," and that, "[Jill is]
passionate about things that are important to her, for example, the struggle of
low-income families and the consequences of that for their education."

In referring to her own leadership, Jill commented that, "I'm interested
in bringing about long-term change. I'm interested in shifting attitudes." Jill
brought her own unique style of feminist leadership to work on social justice
issues, such as those associated with race, class, gender, and poverty. She oozed
formidable energy. In 1996, a newspaper reporter spent a day with a Year 9 class
at Jill's school and wrote a feature article. He introduced Jill to the reader:

> Given those sparky social ingredients [ethnic and socioeconomic mix], if
> this learning establishment was a movie it would probably be *The High
> School From Hell*. The truth is much different. The first bell of the day tolls,
> like Quasimodo's wakeup, at 8:55 A.M., and here comes the principal, a
> charismatic woman called [Jill]. A fully functioning enthusiast, [Jill] is one
> of those human dynamos.

The formidable energy Jill used to bring about change was viewed both positively and negatively by those with whom she worked. "Strong" and "forceful" were words that the staff I interviewed often used to describe Jill's leadership. She was admired for her energy and her capacity for hard work (like the other women in this study, she worked long hours, including weekends). However, a number of staff commented that this was viewed by some staff as daunting, suggesting that, "[Staff] can't keep up with her as she seems superhuman," and that, "Her forcefulness and passion some other people don't find easy to get along with," and "Maybe some might find her overpowering." Because Jill was seen to be working very hard, there was a perceived expectation by staff that they should be working as hard as she did. Even though this was not necessarily the impression that Jill wanted to give, it was what some staff perceived. Two commented that, "[We] cannot keep up with her as she seems superhuman," and "[Jill] can push staff too hard." This was particularly felt by staff who were parents.

Jill often saw solutions to problems very quickly, often more quickly than those with whom she was working. She commented that this led to some tension, as others viewed her as not listening, impatient, or intolerant. This was particularly so when she was stressed. It was common for staff to suggest that it would be helpful if she would reflect and listen more before taking action. They commented that they understood that Jill's actions were not taken for selfish reasons to boost her own status but rather because she had a genuine concern to make a positive difference in the lives of the students and to do it quickly. "[Jill] has great humility, [she is] a selfless person, status doesn't matter as much as doing the job well" (staff member).

## MARIE'S WORK ON COLLABORATIVE DECISION MAKING

Marie also could be uncompromising. This was evident in her belief that others should be consulted and included in decision making.

> . . . considering other points of view, which for me is really important, the points of view of those people who are not as articulate or confident as those people who rush in and let you know straight off how they feel about a particular situation. (Marie)

Marie commented that although some staff might appreciate her personal style of operating, there were also those who would have preferred her to be less waffly and more decisive. There was some staff criticism of her consultative approach, because it took a long time and, like the open-door policy, made it difficult for Marie to get some tasks completed. Marie was adamant about redistributing power to the stakeholders in the decision-making process.

She also was uncompromising about collaborative decision making, even if some staff disagreed with her approach. She resisted their pressure to be more autocratic and suggested that her cultural upbringing had been influential in shaping how she worked with others:

> That's [collaborative decision making] something our whole family believes in, and I think it comes about through my own feminist beliefs. It would have to be a really major crisis for me to say that I'll make that decision quickly.

However, it was Marie's commitment to collaborative decision making that helped resolve the tension she experienced between being Samoan and being feminist. This tension hinged on the emphasis in her culture on respect, the respect for those in authority and those older than oneself. For example, as Marie explains in the following quote, in Samoan culture, it is not proper to question the motives and decisions of those in authority, yet the same constraints are not there for feminists:

> [Y]ou would never question anybody in the family that is older than you, and if you do so, you do so at your own peril and risk being isolated from the family . . . the whole thing of shame and working in such a way that you still leave the person's self-respect intact. I've seen people and sometimes [feminist] women who destroy the self-respect of people through the way they operate.

For Marie, the process of consultation minimized the need for her to challenge and therefore be at odds with her own cultural way of operating. By involving others, the challenges were shared among group members. Because she considered challenging others in authority as disrespectful, she was not prepared to change her commitment to collaborative decision making, even though some found it a tedious way of operating.

Marie commented on how she sometimes had difficulty operating in a mainly white, middle-class educational environment:

> [I]f somebody has said something, what's the use of repeating it again? I don't know if that is something specific to me or whether it is the way I have been brought up to respect that if somebody has already said something that I am undermining them by repeating it and trying to own that argument.

This is dissimilar to the way in which many feminists operate—speaking up and having their say.

## THEME 2—BEING RESPECTED AND SURVIVING

Even though at times staff found the ways of operating of these three women difficult, the women were respected. All three women I studied were public about their feminism, and unlike the women in Joyce's study (1987), they were not treated as a joke but were taken seriously.

The staff enjoyed the clear expectations, and they knew where they stood, as the following comment suggests:

> [Students] see her [Kate's] determination to spend money and provide the resources, they see the improvement. They do not necessarily like what she says, but they respect her for it. The attitude of the whole school is better, more focused, geared towards achievement. The students are settled and content. They know where the boundaries are.

Likewise, Jill was admired for her tenacity in fighting for what she thought was right:

> . . . her spirit of fighting and doing battle for what is right and what she believed in, for example, getting money for students. She did not back down if she believed in something, even if others do not agree. (staff member)

This won Jill friends in the school community, those who felt her empathy for their concerns. "Jill has a powerful body of admiration" (staff member). One staff member, after admitting that Jill was not easy to work with, then went on to comment that she was the best "boss" he had ever had!

Staff respect for Marie also was reflected in their concern for her welfare. On one occasion, when I rang Marie to make an appointment to see her, it was lunchtime and the woman staff member who answered the phone asked if I could ring back so that Marie could finish her lunch without interruption. I frequently heard this concern for Marie's welfare expressed by staff in both casual staff room conversations and in interviews with staff.

So how did these women survive, even thrive, within their institutions when the women in Hollingsworth, Schmuck, and Lock's (1998) study found it necessary to either resign or were pushed out? For the women in this study, the collisions with their respective institutions were minor in comparison, and their collisions were not so close to home. They had a strong body of support from within their own institutions that supported them in their agendas. Each woman also was supported by her board of trustees, and to a great extent, by staff as well.[1] They were not as isolated as I suspect the women in Hollingsworth, Schmuck, and Lock's (1998) study were, and so they were not as vulnerable to being "picked off." This support also acted as a buffer between them and, for example, the parent body in Kate's case, and it allowed them to continue with their transformative agendas. They had chosen their institutions carefully and, like the women in Cooper and others' (in press) study, they had found ways to feel at home in those institutions. It was from this strong base of support that they were able to launch their transformative agendas.

There were other tensions. Even though they were not prepared to conform and be seduced by the new managerialism, at times this created a tension in their working relationships. For Kate and Jill in particular, the tension revolved around how their dominant, strong personalities made them appear to those with whom they were working. This was most evident when they were dealing with an issue they were passionate about. For Marie, the tension she experienced in being both feminist and Samoan was in some part relieved by her insistence on consensual decision making even if, at the same time, that brought her into conflict with some of her own staff.

So in practice, as in theory, the tension was apparent between their feminist leadership agenda and the managerialist agenda. Trying to remain focused on equity without alienating the middle-class caregivers was a difficult balancing act. There is a risk in being too overtly committed to an equity agenda and losing students because of middle-class flight.

At times, as Blackmore (1993) predicted, the women I studied were replacing one mode of power with another similar mode. It was a Catch-22 situation. To drive for change, they were passionate and feisty. Even though their agenda may have been supported by those with whom they worked, those very same qualities also at times made them difficult to work with. As Kenway and Langmead describe in chapter 7, it was emotional labor.

So as Mitchell (1997) suggested, do we expect too much of feminists? Do we expect them to be saints and not do anything wrong? In being feisty, formidable, and determined, the women in the study risked the censure of others. They certainly were not saints. However, many of those with whom they worked, while acknowledging this unsaintliness, at the same time realized the necessity of their single-mindedness to achieve their transformative agendas.

## SUMMARY

This chapter has focused on feminist educational leadership as distinct from women's leadership. I have argued that within a neo-liberal managerialist context of present-day New Zealand feminist principals, such as those I studied, need to be feisty, strong, uncompromising, passionate and determined, and they must have formidable energy if they hope to keep moving forward on social equity issues in their schools. In the three cases focused on in this chapter, the women were able to win the respect of staff and parents as they tried to transform their schools. However, even when staff and parents agreed with the principal's educational value system, they found some of their processes of implementation difficult to cope with, which resulted in a number of tensions. It may be that, unlike the university environments described in the previous chapter, the secondary school environments described here allowed these women to stay in their roles rather than to exit. It may be that they took up different strategies for their feminist action than did the four women described in the previous chapter. Whatever the explanations, clearly feminist leaders in today's climate are well advised to take up the script of the "assertive, uppity woman" described by Erica Jong in the following quote:

> I love being an assertive, uppity woman. What's the alternative? . . . There's no way to be a woman in this world and not be assertive and uppity unless you accept your oppression and just lie down and get into bed in the afternoon. (Mitchell 1997)

## NOTE

1. Boards of trustees are the elected governing bodies of schools.

## REFERENCES

Blackmore, J. 1989. "Educational Leadership: A Feminist Critique and Reconstruction." Pp. 93–129 in *Critical Perspectives on Educational Leadership*, ed. J. Smyth. London: Falmer Press.

Blackmore, J. 1993. *Leadership in Crisis or "a Taste for the Feminine": Feminist Insights into Educational Change.* Geelong: Deakin University, Victoria, Australia.

Codd, J. 1990. "Managerialism: The Problem with Today's Schools." *Delta* 44:17–25.

Codd, J. 1993. "Managerialism, Market Liberalism, and the Move to Self-Managing Schools in New Zealand." Pp. 153–70 in *A Socially Critical View of the Self-Managing School*, ed. J. Smyth. London: Falmer Press.

Cooper, J., M. Benham, M. Collay, A. Martinez-Aleman, and M. Scherr. 2001. *A Famine of Stories: Finding a Home in the Academy.* Albany: State University of New York Press.

Elshtain, J. B. 1987. "Against Androgyny." Pp. 139–59 in *Feminism and Equality*, ed. A. Phillips. Oxford: Basil Blackwell.

Grundy, S. 1993. "Educational Leadership As Emancipatory Praxis." Pp. 165–77 in *Gender Matters in Educational Administration and Policy*, ed. J. Blackmore and J. Kenway. London: Falmer Press.

Hawk, K., and J. Hill. 1997. *Towards Making Achievement Cool.* Paper presented at the New Zealand Association for Research in Education, November 1997.

Hollingsworth, S., P. Schmuck, and R. Lock. 1998. *Women Administrators and the Point of Exit: Collision between the Person and the Institution.* Paper presented at the annual meeting of the American Educational Research Association, April 13–17, San Diego.

James, B., and K. Saville Smith. 1992. "Feminist Perspectives on Complex Organizations." Pp. 31–45 in *The Gender Factor: Women in New Zealand Organizations*, ed. S. Olsson. Palmerston North: Dunmore Press.

Joyce, M. 1987. "Being a Feminist Teacher." Pp. 67–89 in *Teachers: The Culture and Politics of Work*, ed. L. Martin and G. Gerald. London: Falmer Press.

Keown, P., C. McGee, and D. Oliver. 1992. *Monitoring Today's Schools, Report Number 5, National Survey of Secondary Schools*. Hamilton: University of Waikato.

Middleton, S. 1993. *Educating Feminists: Life Histories and Pedagogy*. New York: Teachers College Press.

Mitchell, D., R. Jefferies, P. Keown, and R. McConnell. 1992. "Monitoring Today's Schools: A Scoreboard after 18 Months." Proceedings of the 1st New Zealand Conference on Research in Educational Administration.

Mitchell, S. 1997. *Icons, Saints, and Divas*. Sydney: Harper Collins.

Robertson, J. 1991. *Developing Educational Leadership*. Unpublished master's thesis, University of Waikato, Hamilton, New Zealand.

Robertson, J. 1995. *Principal's Partnerships: An Action Research Study on Professional Development of New Zealand School Principals*. Unpublished doctoral dissertation, University of Waikato, Hamilton, New Zealand.

Spender, D. 1989. *Invisible Women: The Schooling Scandal*. London: Women's Press.

Strachan, J. 1999. "Feminist Educational Leadership in a Neo-Liberal New Zealand Context." *Journal of Educational Administration* 37:2:121–38.

Watson, S., D. Hughes, H. Lauder, R. Strathdee, and I. Simiyu. 1997. "Ethnicity and School Culture." Pp.95–109 in *The New Zealand Annual Review of Education*, ed. I. Livingstone. Wellington: Victoria University of Wellington.

Weedon, C. 1987. *Feminist Practice and Poststructuralist Theory*. Oxford: Blackwell.

Wylie, C. 1994. *Self-Managing Schools in New Zealand: The Fifth Year*. Wellington: New Zealand Council for Educational Research.

Wylie, C. 1995. "Contrary Currents: The Application of the Public Sector Reform Framework in Education." *New Zealand Journal of Educational Studies* 30:2:149–64.

Wylie, C. 1997. *Self-Managing Schools Seven Years On*. Wellington: New Zealand Council for Educational Research.

# Part III

---

## Questioning the Future:
## Feminism, Leadership,
## and Crossing Borders

In this final section, two chapters turn our attention away from the past and present in order to urge us to contemplate the future. Starting with specific discussions about Australia and Canada, both chapters ask us to extrapolate to more global concerns. Questions are raised about how current contexts affect the work that feminists are presently able to do and how their work may be limited even further if certain global trends continue. Inquiries are raised about present and future scenarios for women educational leaders in developing countries, given what has been noted by the authors of previous chapters about women and men as leaders in schools in Western nations.

In chapter 7, Jane Kenway and Dianna Langmead ask, "Is there a future for feminism in the contemporary university?" Drawing on their observations about the "white hot" pace of change in Australian universities, they discuss how features of the postmodern university, which is to "cost the state less and to serve both the state and market forces more," might work to transform feminist knowledge and the work of feminist teachers in universities in the future. Like Reynolds in chapter 2, Kenway and Langmead stress how power relations and configurations of power in the larger context are pivotal to any consideration of women's leadership in schools. Since Reynolds found that feminist activity was a crucial component regarding women's access to leadership roles in elementary and secondary schools, the discussion in chapter 7 begs us to consider how changes in universities could have an impact on women's leadership possibilities at all levels of the schooling system, but especially in universities.

Kenway and Langmead identify five main forms of governmentality in the contemporary Australian university: rationalization, corporatization, marketization, technologization, and globalization. They illustrate how these combine to affect "knowledge work" in the society and knowledge workers such as teachers and administrators in universities. They point out how this environment mitigates against an examination by feminists of the impact of these conditions on women, since the conditions themselves keep most feminists struggling to maintain their current positions and learning how to cope with these new realities. Kenway and Langmead warn, however, that without attention to the larger trends and their possible impacts, feminists may find that gains in terms of policy initiatives and improvements in fostering anti-sexist practices will pass their "shelf life" and either be discarded or become sadly transformed and co-opted. Fortunately, the authors deliver their dire warnings in a humorous parody of a possible version of the future. Beneath the humor is a call to action for all practitioners and researchers who have concerns about women and leadership.

In chapter 8, Deborah Mindorff and Cecilia Reynolds offer concluding thoughts. They look back across the book to explore the two major themes of crossing borders and reconsidering women school leaders as entrepreneurs in today's contexts. They suggest that readers have been urged by the various chapters in this book to reconsider what may have been previously held "comfortable perspectives" about women and school leadership. By setting aside such perspectives, readers have been asked to cross a kind of conceptual border, as they have been presented with studies that span not only a number of countries and offer a view across national borders but studies that also span a number of methods and feminist perspectives.

In this concluding chapter, Mindorff and Reynolds revisit the term *entrepreneurship* and examine some specific examples of how an "entrepreneurial mind-set" and the "social entrepreneur" might be fruitful concepts as we strive to rethink school leadership and gender in today's contexts.

The chapter and the book conclude with an invitation to readers to consider how they, as potential or actual leaders in schools, can use critical thought to prepare for strategic and tactical decisions about future research and action and about shaping and being shaped by the worlds they construct and have the power to change.

CHAPTER SEVEN

# Is There a Future for Feminism in the Contemporary University?

Jane Kenway and Dianna Langmead

*Australia*

## INTRODUCTION

In this chapter[1] we examine the dominant forces that are shaping academic life for women in Australia and in many other so-called developed "Western" countries. Our first question is, "What is the current context for feminists who work in universities?" Our second and related question is, "What effect might this context have on the future of feminists in academe and on the work they are able to do?" We address these questions by examining the literature on higher education to identify the main forms of "governmentality" evidenced by new policies and practices. We also consider what the current feminist literature on women in universities has to say. Our examination leads to a discussion of likely scenarios and a tongue-in-cheek description of "designer feminisms" suitable to an era of marketization and globalization. We conclude by briefly alluding to some implications for women leaders at all levels in education.

## GOVERNMENTALITY AND THE "NOW" UNIVERSITY

The current pace of change in university education in Australia is "white hot." The fierce and recent debate in the popular press and in the literature on higher education in Australia (see, e.g., Coady 2000; Smith 1996) makes it clear that

129

current university policies vary in significant ways from those that predominat-ed in the 1970s and early 1980s. Beneath a welter of policy rhetoric the key messages appear to be that universities are to cost the state less and to serve both the state and market forces more.[2] Many (see, e.g., James 2000) have argued that this indicates that the triumph of economics over university education is now complete. Such literature suggests that this triumph is manifest in six particular forms of "governmentality," or what Foucault calls the "conduct of conduct." These forms are rationalization, corporatization, marketization, vocationaliza-tion, technologization, and globalization. First, then, we mention each of these terms and give examples of how each is evident in the current university sec-tor in Australia.

The first form of governmentality under discussion here is *rationalization*. It is visible when reductions in government funding lead universities to "down-size" and to look for nonstate sources of funds in an effort to increase what has been called their "flexibility." Most universities seem to be striving for this new form of flexibility by "rationalizing" their academic and support staff. In Australia, like many countries around the globe, there is increasing evidence that older, tenured staff members are being encouraged to retire, to take "vol-untary redundancy" or they are made redundant. One result of this is that a larger percentage of university staff is being hired on a sessional basis and can be declared "peripheral" rather than "core" workers in higher education insti-tutions. The literature (Blackmore and Angwin 1996; Cox, 1995; Filmer, 1997) indicates that the employment of casual or part-time labor may have the para-doxical effect of actually intensifying rather than diminishing the work of the "core" workers. Core, part-time, and casual workers in existing settings are all encouraged by the institution to work harder, faster, and "smarter." But overall, there are fewer people to do more work. The name of the game is lean pro-duction and, as the Tertiary Education Union makes clear, the intensification of work is accompanied by the intensification of stress, workplace bullying, and a serious decline in morale and workers' health and well-being (Advocate 2000). In her earlier chapter, Young observes a similar pattern in elementary and sec-ondary schools in Alberta, Canada. Resource management has increasingly become the educational bottom line.

The second form of governmentality is *corporatization*. This means that business management principles, previously few in public service organizations, are now being applied to and by university management (Duncan 2000). Increasingly less, academic staff are involved in the real work of university gov-ernance. Indeed, the notion of academic staff as stakeholders in the governance of the university has been superceded by the view that the main stakeholders are business and industry. In fact, the representation and influence of business and industry on universities' governing bodies are increasing. In contrast, acad-emic staff are "drip fed" information largely on a "need to know" basis. Codes of silence or "cultures of secrecy" have emerged, associated with notions of "commercial in confidence" that are seen to apply to more and more university activity. Due process in this context is redefined. Further, in the interests of the "corporate" image, members of academic staff are discouraged from and even punished for commenting critically in public on matters internal to their university or, indeed, on the changing nature of the university sector. At the same time, internal dissent also is frowned upon. As Duncan (2000) notes, "The supporters of justice, fairness, and open processes are transmuted somehow into forces of conservatism, museum pieces standing in the way of modernization and neat managerial development" (62). This has implications for the knowledge work of the university, which at its best has conventionally been underpinned by the principles of open and critical intellectual inquiry and free speech or, as Duncan (2000) calls it, "independence, diversity, and disputatiousness" (62). As he argues, efficiency and effectiveness are not incompatible with such traditions, but current modes of corporatization are.

University corporatization often involves contradictory moves. A simultaneous movement toward decentralization and recentralization, for instance, is a core aspect of university governance. There also have been mixed messages about such things as the autonomy and accountability of the university from and to the state. Within institutions with centralized budget responsibility, stress and crisis are still passed "down the line" to be dealt with by employees who have little or no say in budget allocations. Newly "flattened hierarchies" can still be observed to have a clearly hierarchical command structure where accountability runs either steeply upward (Coleman 1995, 108) or outward—to "clients" via an increased emphasis on student assessment of teaching or the university's capacity to ensure students' employment.

Based on the application of business management principles, and drawing strength from the corporate world's public stigmatization of academics and the unworldliness of their work, individual academic output is subject to intensified performance appraisal, often using performance indicators and quality audits developed by an expanding cadre of administrative staff in new managerial units (Watts 2000). Such performance indicators are then often used in the process of institutional and individual "self-boosting" (Manne 2000). This has particular implications for the relationships between those who work in academic settings. The more we measure the input and output of academic workers, the more we encourage them to understand themselves as autonomous individuals who must compete against colleagues, both as individuals and as members of a group[3]. When we combine this competitive stance with dramatically increased workloads and higher expectations in teaching, research, and administrative work, it is highly likely that we will find a divided academic staff rather than a collegial community. To the extent that they existed in the past (and for a debate on this, see Cassidy 1998), collegiality and trust are rapidly being replaced by cultures characterized by distrust and anxiety. Under such circumstances, control is increasingly gained by edict, or it is based on a fear of reprisal. Individuals are encouraged to internalize the new business discourses that support and maintain corporatization as an acceptable and even a desirable form of governance in the academic realm.

Indeed, many now talk of two cultures in conflict in the academy. These are not the sciences and the humanities as C. P. Snow once observed, but rather the academics involved in research and teaching and the managers and their administrative staff—what Manne (2000, 17) calls "a separate caste of university administrators." He argues that "a wall of mutual incomprehension" separates them. One example of such separation pertains to notions of quality or excellence that have tended to become empty, self-referential disciplining signifiers. They bare little relationship to what Giovanni Carsaniga in Smith (1996, 111) calls the "academic ecology," which includes good libraries, accommodation and amenities, and space and time to think, read, and write. At the apex of the management culture are members of the senior management group who are often cocooned from the everyday worlds and work of their organization by the privileges they accrue to themselves as they take on the status of their CEO "peers" in the corporate world.

*Marketization* is the third strategy of governmentality identified in the literature on current universities (The Australian Universities Review—Special Issue on Marketization 1993). It proceeds hand in glove with corporatization and *vocationalization*, which is the fourth strategy. Under marketization, user-pay schemes and quasi-voucher schemes[4] are multiplying, and universities are going further and further afield to find new sources of income. Academic "entrepreneurs" roam an increasingly wide range of "developing" countries in search of the lucrative education export dollar. As Hall suggests in a previous chapter, entrepreneurship in education need not be seen as a problem in itself. However, the literature on higher education (see, e.g., Filmer 1997) has identified a number of problematic outcomes from international university entrepreneurship. We now see a whole new set of developments such as onshore and offshore partnerships and subsidiaries in the academy. And it often is the case that these are run for profit in order to cross-subsidize the university for the loss of government money. Internationalizing the curriculum in the ways outlined by Rizvi and Walsh (1998) and implied in Marginson's (2000) discussions of "living with the other" is a poor second to marketing the product to potential client/students via the logic of what Watts calls "brochure speak." This, he says, employs the impoverished language and morality of the public relations and advertising world. In such a world, face value and best face matter more than substance—image is all. Using the discourse of the market, students frequently view themselves and are viewed by others as "investing" in a university education. The payment of fees intensifies the notion of education as a commodity and of customer rights of student "consumers." This feeds into a corporate model of the university that has the potential to shift the weight of responsibility for learning from a student/teacher partnership to the academic instructor or teacher alone (Coleman 1995, 108).

Critics of the trend toward marketization have pointed to counterproductive ways in which universities are increasingly turning to business and industry for research and teaching sponsorship and even for funding to create specific programs. (Deakin University's program for the Coles supermarket chain is an infamous example.) An effect is that universities often seek to redefine themselves according to the preferences and needs of business and industry. Vocationalization and commercialization are the twin peaks of what some have called the "big business" agenda within academe.

*Vocationalization* has serious implications for those bodies of knowledge that find it difficult to "rebadge" themselves as vocational (i.e., as assisting students to be "job ready"). And even when they try to do so, such bodies of knowledge as history and the humanities still tend to be residualized, as recent debates in the higher education supplement of the major Australian newspaper, *The Australian*, indicate. As centers of learning, modern universities have conventionally valued disciplinary diversity and balance. This is no longer the case, as universities' "missions" are increasingly oriented toward the empty ambitions associated with such vacuous notions as "world's best practice." Faculties that can generate sizable income are not expected to "cross-subsidize" those that cannot, in the interests of the general good of the university, the university sector, and the culture more broadly. Rather, they are encouraged to pursue unlimited growth without regard to the wider implications. Further, as Duncan (2000, 58) points out, "Many a VC (Vice Chancellor) suffers from the well-known Edifice Complex, and would prefer a new piece of real estate to the salvation of a discipline."

The most valued research in this context is applied "end user" research, conducted in partnership with "industry" with the potential for commercialization. Indeed, in Australia, the Commonwealth Minister for Education has just introduced legislation to increase ministerial power over government funding for research, whereas until now, independent bodies have recommended funding on a merit basis. Further, the minister also seeks to make it possible for nonuniversity bodies to compete with universities for government research money, thus subjecting research funding to "the competitive market" (Wells 2000a). Indeed, this is a first step in the minister's program of regulated deregulation that seeks to "break down the distinction between "public" and "private" universities and to open up Australian universities to a global free trade in educational services" (Wells 2000b, 46).

Most universities now have one (or more) commercial arm, and they regularly "benchmark" against each other with regard to income from student fees and other sources (BJ 1997). Indeed, income generation tends to be treated as a product in its own right. Merit for faculty members and the institutions themselves is redefined accordingly, sometimes through league tables in the press. Teaching and research are coming to be regarded as baseline activities. Staff are expected to "add value" by gaining various lucrative consultancies and by doing other deals. Those who do not do so among the core academic staff are implicitly understood as asset strippers—drawing their pay but not bringing in resources. Ironically, there is a growing perception that the university's "core" workers are not its academic staff but its managers and marketers who know how to "work smart in the real world."

In today's world, universities are increasingly coming to understand themselves as direct economic agencies of the state, as opposed to ideological apparatuses of the state, with regard to questions of reason and culture, as argued by Bill Readings in his book *The University in Ruins* (cited in Smith 1996). As such, they are expected to enhance the state's "capacity building" work and thus to gear university activities toward directly supporting productivity gains, enhancing international competitiveness, and creating an ideological climate of support for "missions" sanctioned and encouraged by the state. As they continue along the path of hypercompetitiveness and continuous improvement set out in the marketization discourse just discussed, *technologization* and *globalization*, understood in neo-liberal terms, are key features of the scenario and predictably will play a large part in reshaping the contemporary university. These are the fifth and sixth forms of governmentality under discussion in this chapter.

The literature that is critical of these two forms of governmentality predicts that in the future, universities will understand themselves as, and take on the features of, global corporations. Witness the following quotation from a promotional flyer for a conference held at the Royal Melbourne Institute of Technology in 1997:

> In the context of a rapidly internationalizing global economy presenting new challenges for cultures, economies, and technology, the world's universities are being faced with decisions about how they operate in a borderless world. . . . Easier movement of populations between countries, regional economic cooperation, and new technologies are increasing competition to provide faster, better, and more relevant education. . . . In effect, universities are reinventing themselves as dynamic service providers, as well as traditional teaching, learning, and research centres. (R.M.I.T. University 1997, 3)

Interestingly, the more universities see themselves as "players" in global education techno-markets, the more their relationship to the particular territories and sovereignties of their origins becomes problematic. It may well be the case that in reinventing themselves internationally, universities may move away from state "capacity-building" work and orient themselves more toward global, regional, or local interests instead (Rizvi and Walsh 1998; Smith 1996).

Two recent developments point strongly to one possible direction here. These are called Universitas 21 and the Global University Alliance. The former involves an alliance between a network of eighteen universities from ten countries and Rupert Murdoch's News Corporation. Further, as Fitzclarence (2000) points out, Universitas 21 "enrolls 500,000 students, employs approximately 44,000 academics and researchers, and has a combined operating budget of $U.S.9 billion." The argument is made that Murdoch's ambitions to gain a strong foothold in the potentially lucrative market of e-education are enhanced by attaching his companies to a prestigious international alliance of universities. On the other hand, universities argue that the alliance will help replenish their coffers by moving them away from relying on public funding and will help them diversify pedagogy and commercialize intellectual property. But much else seems to be at stake here. As pointed out at the Transnational Education Symposium in Melbourne in November 2000, such practices of borderless education raise questions about the future investment of public/state money in internationalized and increasingly privatized universities. They also threaten to further compromise intellectual freedom and independence, not to mention universities' integrity and credibility as sources of disinterested knowledge produced by the "best possible thinking and practice" in the public good (Seddon 1999). Further questions arise here about how quality, academic accreditation, and appropriate governance come to be understood in this context and the extent to which knowledge in this context can be localized. And what are the implications for academic workers?

Technologically supported lean production methods go hand in hand with widespread business practices such as subcontracting, outsourcing, and customizing. Indeed, the deterritorialized virtual university is a popular fantasy among many university managers who see themselves as core workers and view academics as disposable. It is possible that place-bound, classroom-bound workers such as university teachers will be increasingly marginalized as esteem and money increasingly flow to the top end of the corporate university. The internationally connected producers of the knowledge most valued in the corporate sector, those who can provide "information differentials" (Weber 1996, 62), will hold sway. Indeed, one overarching question here is about the place and purpose of university education in the twenty-first century, and another is, "Do equity and diversity still have a place, or are they to be sacrificed to the global market in e-education?" What are the implications, then, of such a scenario for the construction and production of knowledge itself?

## KNOWLEDGE IN THE CONTEMPORARY UNIVERSITY

Clearly, the university has evolved over time and space in response to changing economic and cultural circumstances. Equally clearly, universities are diverse—there is no one idea of the university, as the contributors to Smith (1996) emphasize. Nonetheless, there are certain ideals that many still associate with the university that involve holding much in tension, including tradition and innovation, closure and openness, and the divergent and interdependent tendencies associated with acquiring both established and new knowledge. These ideals then include passing on knowledge and the pursuit of new knowledge. In the best traditions of this ideal, this happens in a disinterested manner and informs social progress. In addition, as Patton in Smith (1996) argues, universities also are expected to encourage "the exercise of critical judgement on matters of public importance." For instance, under the previous welfare economy, universities were implicated within public policies that involved some state intervention against the market and in the interests of social justice and the common good (Lingard 1997, 5). Historically, the state funding and state philosophies noted above ensured that universities had a certain autonomy and authority to pursue knowledge according to their own designs and in accordance with the norms associated with the curriculum and pursuit of knowledge. Now, in contrast, Lingard argues that there is less intervention from the state in the interests of justice and the common good, and instead the state underwrites the market economy. The move in power relations is from a "social nexus" to a "cash nexus" (Weber 1996, 39). Dependence on state funds and on new state philosophies has actually compromised universities' autonomy. The state now expects universities to galvanize "the economic potential of knowledge" (Symes, in McCollow and Lingard 1996, 16). University education has come to be seen as an industry with attendant expectations of efficiency, utility, and economic returns. It is becoming less and less likely to be seen as providing a public service with intangible social benefits, as a source of enlightenment, and as a contributor to the critical, cultural, aesthetic, and liberal democratic sensibilities of the state. Specifically, new state influences have meant that academics are to become corporate and market professionals (McCollow and Lingard 1996, 12–16), in other words, "knowledge workers."

KNOWLEDGE WORKERS

In the general literature on knowledge workers, academics are seldom identified, even though generating various forms of intellectual capital is their stock in trade. Indeed, Weber (1996) makes clear how knowledge is conceived, acquired, transmitted, and practiced and reveals what the work of the university academic is largely about. Nonetheless, Drucker (1995) and Stewart (1997) ignore academics. However, university academics are now being reconstructed as knowledge workers. Knowledge workers are those who apply established intellectual and scientific skills in work geared to the ends laid down by the owners or controllers of large-scale industrial and administrative complexes (Sharp and White 1968, 30). Professors as knowledge workers fit Stewart's (1997) notion of a labor elite. A potential irony here is that universities' intellectual capital depends on a critical interrogation of knowledge from various points of view and many different sets of interests. Without such critical friction, knowledge may stagnate, and the university may have less to offer its "clients."

It would appear that universities are no longer expected or expect to pursue the critical interrogation of knowledge for its own sake and for the greater good. The status of such knowledge in the current context is ambiguous. One could speculate that if such knowledge is able to assist the university achieve some aspects of its corporate goals, then it would have no objection to it. However, one could also surmise that the university would not go out on a limb to protect such knowledge if it were at cross-purposes with its corporate goals. The university might well either let such knowledge languish or actively seek to repress it.

Of course, many academics, among them many feminists, continue to believe that universities are places where there should be a critical interrogation. Such an interrogation creates knowledge that is "disinterested," that is, knowledge that is for its own sake, or in the interests of what Giddens (1994) calls emancipatory and life politics. Are feminists and other academics who continue to believe in the value of disinterested knowledge in universities now "alternative" or "oppositional" members of the academic staff? What happens to them in the new division of labor in academe?

## WOMEN WHO DO KNOWLEDGE WORK

What does the feminist literature have to say about new modes of governmentality and knowledge work? Recently, feminists have "investigated the gap between [the] model of equality and academic fairness and the sexist reality of the academy" (Brooks 1997, 1). Having looked within the university at the operations and processes of power, as well as how academic women are located within these processes and how they experience them, feminists have documented the following patterns of discrimination, disadvantage, and differentiation for academic women:

1. The biases that reflect male dominance in academic knowledge and practice (Brooks 1997, 130). In the 1960s, Jessie Bernard divided the university faculty into teachers and "men-of-knowledge." Teachers, she argued, are instruments of communication; "men-of-knowledge" are authors of knowledge. She observed that teachers in academe are usually female, while "men-of-knowledge" are usually male (in Simeone 1987, 52).

2. The difficulties for women academics of coordinating the demands of two "greedy institutions"—university and family (Acker 1994, 126).

3. The invisibility or extra-visibility of women in universities. This comes about largely because a persistent underrepresentation of women in many disciplines often means that female academics must manage relations with their male colleagues from a minority or token position (Acker 1994, 127–28).

4. The lingering perception in academic settings, that women are mainly support workers and educational consumers, not educational decision makers (Ramsay 1995, 91).

5. The persistent onus on women faculty members to take the initiative in setting up Equal Employment Opportunities policies or programs and to foster feminist approaches to educational reform (Arnot and Barton 1992, 50).

6. The differential effects of all of the above on notions of merit for men and women in the academy. Such differences affect the promotion routes of men and women who work in the university (Allen and Castleman 1995, 20–30).

In general, this body of feminist literature exposes the persistently "chilly climate" of university cultures for women. The argument is that, in the past, women academics have had to deal with exclusion, exploitation, and discrimination. This has meant that when women have been knowledge workers, they often have faced career limitations and cultural entrenchment.

What do feminists say about current contexts? They suggest that organizational micro-politics within universities may be further undermining women and women's knowledge (Morley and Walsh 1995). Along with their male counterparts, female academics are experiencing alienation and frustration. They feel overworked and devalued, despite high levels of achievement and institutional commitment (Butler and Schulz 1995, 38–57). Indeed, today's climate may be fostering a debasement of women's place in the restructured organization and a decline in working conditions, marked by lower rates of pay and fewer tenured positions, signs of what could be called the "feminization" of teaching (Blackmore and Angwin 1996; Probert 1998). Blackmore (1997, 93) has argued that all of this has created enhanced opportunities for some individuals and institutions to mobilize their "politics of advantage" and so to overwhelm notions of gender equity. Acker (1994, 133) has pointed to the importance of understanding the gender implications of current contexts, while Butler and Schulz (1995, 55) have argued that, given the current climate of uncertainty and massive change within higher education in Australia, it is an "open moment" for women to transform the culture and structures of universities. Eva Cox (1995, 69–70) calls for a vision beyond Equal Employment Opportunities and women's studies that involves a "feminist redesign of the whole system."

While we commend the fighting spirit of such views, given the discussion of the complex elements of governmentality we have already outlined in this chapter, we feel that the feminist authors such as those we have quoted may be too optimistic. Clearly, the chillier climate of current times makes institutional redesign in the interests of gender justice even more difficult than in the past. Perhaps we now need to examine the implications of these new conditions for feminists themselves, and for the future of different forms of feminism within the academy. Are feminist academics all so busy working smart and working fast that they have no time to examine these implications? What can we see when we take the time to do so?

## FEMINISTS AS "KNOWLEDGE WORKERS" IN UNIVERSITIES

Given the not-too-bright picture for women academics, which we have described, how are feminist "knowledge workers" and feminist knowledge itself (within academia) going to hold up in the face of the new forms of governmentality?

In one scenario, all women academics, simply by belonging to their gender group, may be drawn yet further into the vortex of the increasingly "needy and greedy" institutions of university and family. As in the wider society, when welfare and service are reprivatized, the emotional labor of women in the academy may intensify despite the wishes or preferences of individual women. According to this scenario, feminist academics may find themselves working under conditions that are increasingly hostile to their feminist pedagogies and their efforts to construct feminist knowledge. Feminism itself may be repositioned as merely a support site where women meet to develop strategies for dealing with structural and other difficulties.

In a further scenario, the possibilities of intensified teaching and marginalized research may mean a return to the days of women teachers and "men of knowledge." This is a dangerous scenario for feminists in the academy, because knowledge production is crucial to keeping feminism alive and relevant. Indeed, as our discussion of governmentality within the university has indicated, a wide array of new lines of inquiry for feminists has emerged. Let us examine some quick examples.

Just as feminists reworked the notions of citizen and the state in the 1970s and 1980s, so they must now rework notions of the market, the global, the national, and the local. Just as feminists reworked notions of politics and activism in the 1970s and 1980s, they must now rework such notions in alignment with the new paradigms of governmentality. These paradigms entail problematic views of individualism, new configurations of time and space, and the rise of a "third sector" (Rifkin 1995) that includes non-government organizations (NGOs) and supranational agencies. Feminist reworkings will need to recognize both the potential and the limits of legislation and litigation at the state and institutional levels (Sassen 1996). Further, just as feminists deconstructed and reworked the academic canons of the last three decades, so they now must deconstruct the "informational" canons currently being formed. These new canons include those associated with digital entrepreneurialism and the tyranny of the virtual circle between capital and technology. Feminist globalization literature on work, place, embodiment, experience, and migration flows must be complemented with a feminist analysis of networks of power, particularly as these apply to knowledge workers and teachers, not only in universities but also in elementary and secondary schools.

While new forms of governmentality can open up new and important lines of inquiry for feminist research, these new forms can simultaneously close down feminists' opportunities to undertake such inquiry in universities. At this stage, it is not at all clear which feminists and which feminisms will survive the commercialization and commodification of knowledge in the global intellectual/economic bazaar.

What economic utility within the currently reconfigured university is there for forms of feminist knowledge that oppose economic rationalism and globalization based on their attendant discriminatory and debilitating effects for women's economic, political, and citizenship rights? What economic utility is there for gender-inclusive models of scholarship and management?

Clearly, if feminism and feminists align themselves with social-democratic philosophies and against economic rationalism and liberal-individualist philosophies, feminist knowledge is not likely to be popular in universities desperately seeking resources and funding from radically conservative governments and from commercial sources. How many private sponsors are likely to provide funds to ensure that feminist knowledge remains in the academy? Indeed, are such sponsors likely to withhold funds to those universities that harbor uncomfortable forms of feminist knowledge?

The current context puts feminism in an awkward position for other reasons as well. In the past, feminists helped expose the gender, class, ethnic, and sexual biases in notions of the common good. They revealed the interests at play in seemingly "disinterested" forms of knowledge, and they laid bare the inequality and injustice in what had previously been construed as fair practices and policies. In a sense, then, feminists have always been oppositional knowledge workers within universities, challenging the tenets of established disciplines and practices. There is a paradox here for feminists.

On the one hand, feminists within universities have tended to be critical of the enlightenment traditions evident in the university. On the other hand, they have been somewhat dependent on these very traditions as the notion that the university must have a certain critical distance from society, economy, and culture for it to do its interpretive and critical work. The time and resources necessary for enlightenment notions about the leisurely pursuit of knowledge and the opportunity to develop rich pedagogies are at risk in the corporate university with its obsession with speed and utility. It is not at all clear what meta-discourses feminists can employ here to defend feminism within the corporate university with its strong ties to the neo-liberal state and global economy. We might well ask, then, do feminists want to become conventional knowledge workers and be assimilated into the world of intellectual capital? Let us resort to parody for a moment.

## WHAT IS THE SHELF LIFE OF FEMINISM IN THE CONTEMPORARY UNIVERSITY?

Feminist work at the policy and administrative levels within the university has been most visible to date in the form of Affirmative Action (AA), EEO poli-

cies and calls for anti-sexist practices for students and staff within the organization. It seems to us that in Australia, both AA and EEO have passed their use-
by date, at least when it comes to having any practical effects (Blackmore 2000).
As a consequence of restructuring, these policies and their implementation
have been pushed to the very back of the shelf. They have been given a great
deal of bad press, and there have been numerous attacks on political correctness
and "victim" feminism. It seems that accountability required by legislation is
the only reason EEO and AA policies remain on the Australian shelf at all.
Having lost most of their purchasing value, they can be viewed as image built
on image built on image—with an imaginary relationship to the real university world of "Boys R Us." The policies themselves often conceal the "real."

And what of feminist courses and feminist pedagogy? What is their shelf
life in the leaner, fee-charging world of uni-business? To the extent that feminist courses attract shoppers—they are shoppers with little money—this does
not auger well for postgraduate programs. With the increasing commodification of knowledge, it also is increasingly likely that undergraduate feminist
courses will lose their market share. Viewed instrumentally, these feminist
undergraduate courses may be seen as a bad investment! The tongue-in-cheek
answer to this marketing problem is designer feminism. Some possible course
titles borrowed from the discourses of marketing and management follow:

Women's Ways of Budgeting
Downsizing without Pain through Aromatherapy
Total Quality Femininity
Performing Your Feminine Indicators
Multi-skilling Women: Combining Out-work and House-work
Auditing Your Image: How to Dress for Success
Lean Production: Diets on the Dole
Terminal Relationships and Digital Dalliances: Dating at Your Desk

The designer line also could have some of these more theoretical courses as well:

Downsizing Derrida
Flexible Foucault
Lacan and Lean Production
Drucker and Disembodiment
Feminist Ethics, Freud, and the Fluid Firm
Postmodernism and Privatization

Feminist pedagogy, however, is likely to be regarded as a luxury item, one
that universities cannot afford. It is considered a fat pedagogy—too resource
consuming. Anorexic pedagogies are better for the health of the budget.

Marked down, flexible feminism is what will be required: mass-produced courses sold on-line (Dial-a-Feminist) or sold off the shelf. "McFeminism" will be what characterizes undergraduate courses: feminist fast food for thought. At this stage, it is not at all clear how Western feminist courses can be packaged and marketed offshore. Indeed, only a feminism with a postcolonial designer label could be legitimately sold in the global education bazaar. "Kentucky Fried Feminism" is not acceptable.

Feminist research may have more and more difficulty attracting sponsors and may be increasingly conducted in university sweatshops—unfunded or poorly funded. In a marketized educational environment, traditional feminist sales pitches do not sell well. Feminism's moral agenda is viewed as a fashion story of a few seasons ago. Feminism in the academy is overstocked, going cheap. It is yesterday's bread, the stale, throwaway consequence of unplanned obsolescence, because no preservatives were added. "Serve yourself—serves you right" could be the attitude of university administrators as they pump money into more reliable brand names such as Commerce, Law, and Information Technology. Solid investments—no speculation required—just pay your money and collect your frequent (high) flyer points.

What of power relations within feminism itself? Are feminists becoming absorbed within global market relations? Are feminists erecting trade barriers? Are "femocrats" in the well-stocked exchange doing insider trading? Is the "American Feminist Express" colonizing the globe? Might we expect global feminist franchises such as Butler Boutiques, de Lauretis Delis, or Haraway's Hardware? "When the going gets tough, the tough go shopping."

## IMPLICATIONS FOR WOMEN AND SCHOOL LEADERSHIP

Clearly, the times and the contemporary university raise a host of new issues for feminists in the academy. Feminism's survival may be at stake. We would perhaps be well advised to "go shopping" for new ideas about how to secure a future for feminism and feminists in the academy. But what might all of this mean for school leadership?

As other chapters of this book indicate, there are intricate ties between the ideas and activities of feminists in elementary and secondary schools and feminists in the university sector. Yet women who take on official leadership roles around the globe at various levels within educational systems have often actively rejected the feminist label. Despite this, evidence strongly suggests that gender relations within school organizations and within the various scripts available to men and women in society (Oerton 1996) continue to require further study from a feminist perspective if we are to continue to deepen our understanding of school leadership. Equally, people in school leadership roles still usually come to their positions in the schooling sector via university education. If, as we have speculated here, only a hollow form of quasi-feminism were to survive in the universities of the future, then there would be a number of repercussions for both men and women as "knowledge workers" in the schooling sector.

In offering this account of the reculturing and restructuring of universities, we also offer school leaders a cautionary tale and remind them and university leaders of the importance of intersectoral vigilance. As indicated throughout this book, schools are not immune from the modes of governmentality that have both consumed contemporary universities and led them to lose a strong sense of their educational purposes. The question "What is the end to which university and school education is the means?" gets continually lost in pursuit of reputation and the "bottom line." As we have shown, university managers have adopted the false certainty of corporate consensus and overregulation. But as all good educational leaders and teachers know, education only flourishes in an environment that stimulates new ideas, dissident views, debates, and critiques in the context of mutual respect and trust. Indeed, Reading's notion of a "community of dissensus" (in Smith 1996, 70) seems a more apt model of community building for educational leaders to pursue.

The authors of the previous chapters have offered critical comments about some unintended outcomes and the "roadblocks" encountered by women in school leadership. In so doing, they have tried to sustain an ongoing debate about gender and school leadership in ways that will have an impact on policies and practices in schools. The enormity of the task of mounting and sustaining that debate is made clear in our discussion of contemporary university culture. As we have argued, universities are being restructured according to trends in the larger culture and in ways that may make the task of addressing gender issues in school leadership at all levels even more difficult in the future. Like others in this book, we recognize that men and women can pick up political and economic scripts and enact them in creative and powerful ways. Our hope is that they can do so informed and supported by a vibrant, self-reflexive feminist community whose members remain at the cutting edge within universities around the world. As Brown (1996) says, "As well as preserving the knowledge and traditions of society, universities must challenge its assumptions and make it confront its future." School leaders must do no less.

## NOTES

1. An earlier version of this paper was published in Hancock (1999, 192–205).

2. For the triennium of 1999–2001, over one billion $A of public funding to public universities is to be cut.

3. It is worth noting in this context that although Australian scientists are publishing more, they appear to be reading less—according to the Citation Indices (Roberts, 2000).

4. See Wells (2000b) for a discussion of the manner in which a quasi-voucher scheme is now applied to research students.

## REFERENCES

Acker, S. 1994. *Gendered Education.* Buckingham: Open University Press.

*Advocate.* 2000. Journal of the National Tertiary Education Union 7:5 (November): 19.

Allen, M., and T. Castleman. 1995. "Gender Privilege in Higher Education: Examining Its Dimensions and Dynamics." Pp. 20–30 in *Women, Culture, and Universities: A Chilly Climate?*, ed. A. M. Payne and L. Shoemark. Sydney: University of Technology, Sydney, Women's Forum.

Arnot, M., and L. Barton, eds. 1992. *Voicing Concerns: Sociological Perspectives on Contemporary Education Reforms.* Oxfordshire: Triangle Books.

*The Australian Universities Review—Special Issue on Marketization.* 1993. Vol. 36, No. 2, pp. 2–54.

BJ. 1997. "UTS Tops Fee-Paying Students." *Campus Review* 7:24:5.

Blackmore, J. 1997. "Disciplining Feminism: A Look at Gender-Equity Struggles in Australian Higher Education." Pp. 75–98 in *Dangerous Territories: Struggles for Difference and Equality in Education*, ed. L. Roman and L. Eyre. New York: Routledge.

Blackmore, J., and J. Angwin. 1996. *Educational Outworkers: Emerging Issues for Women Educators in the Restructured Tertiary Educational Labor Market.* Geelong: Deakin Center for Education and Change.

Blackmore, J. 2000. "'Hanging onto the Edge': An Australian Case Study of Women, Universities, and Globalization." Pp. 333–53 in *Globalization and Education: Integration and Contestation across Cultures*, ed. N. Stromquist and K. Monkman. Lanham, Md.: Rowman and Littlefield.

Brooks, A. 1997. *Academic Women.* Buckingham: Open University Press.

Brown, G. 1996. "2000 and Beyond—The University of the Future." In *Ideas of the University, Research, Research Institute for the Humanities and Social Sciences*, ed. T. Smith. Sydney: University of Sydney, with Power Publications.

Butler, E., and L. Schulz. 1995. "Women and the Politics of University Work: An Agenda for the Organization." Pp. 38–57 in *Women, Culture, and Universities: A Chilly Climate?*, ed. A. M. Payne and L. Shoemark. Sydney: University of Technology, Sydney Women's Forum.

Cassidy, B. 1998. "Hierarchy and Collegiality in Australian Universities." In *The Australian Universities Review—Special Issue Higher Education and the Politics of Difference* 41:2:43–49.

Coady, T., ed. 2000. *Why Universities Matter.* Sydney: Allen & Unwin.

Coleman, K. 1995. "Women and Corporate Management in Universities." Pp. 106–15 in *Women, Culture, and Universities: A Chilly Climate?*, ed. A. M. Payne and L. Shoemark. Sydney: University of Technology, Sydney Women's Forum.

Cox, E. 1995. "Gender Privilege in Higher Education: Examining Its Dimensions and Dynamics." Pp. 68–73 in *Women, Culture, and Universities: A Chilly Climate?*, ed. A. M. Payne and L. Shoemark. Sydney: University of Technology, Sydney Women's Forum.

Drucker, P. 1995. *Managing in an Age of Great Change.* Oxford: Butterworth-Heinemann.

Duncan, G. 2000. "Notes from a Departed Dean." In *The Australian Universities Review—Special Issue Higher Education and the Politics of Difference* 41:2:55–63.

Filmer, P. 1997. "Disinterestedness and the Modern University." Pp. 48–58 in *The Postmodern University? Contested Visions of Higher Education in Society*, ed. A. Smith and F. Webster. Buckingham: SRHE and Open University Press.

Fitzclarence, L. 2000. "The Bonfire of the Universities." *Arena Magazine* 48 (September): 46–50.

Giddens, A. 1994. *Beyond Left and Right: The Future of Radical Politics.* Stanford, Calif.: Stanford University Press.

Hancock, L., ed. 1999. *Women, Public Policy, and the State.* South Yarra, Victoria: Macmillan.

James, P., ed. 2000. *Burning Down the House: The Bonfire of the Universities.* Melbourne: Association for the Public University, with Arena Publications.

Lingard, B. 1997. "The Problematic Coalition of Markets and Social Justice." *Education Links* 54:4–7.

Manne, R. 2000. "The Death of the University." Pp. 16–20 in *Burning Down the House: The Bonfire of the Universities*, ed. P. James. Melbourne: Association for the Public University, with Arena Publications.

Marginson, S. 2000. "Living with the Other: Higher Education in the Global Era." In *Australian Universities Review* 12:2:5–9.

McCollow, J., and B. Lingard. 1996. "Changing Discourses and Practices of Academic Work." *Australian Universities Review* 39:2:11–19.

Morley, L., and V. Walsh, eds. 1995. *Breaking Boundaries: Women in Higher Education (Gender and Higher Education Miniseries).* London: Taylor & Francis.

Oerton, S. 1996. *Beyond Hierarchy: Gender, Sexuality, and the Social Economy.* London: Taylor & Francis.

Probert, B. 1998. "Working in Australian Universities: Pay Equity for Men and Women?" *Australian Universities Review* 41:2:33–42.

Ramsay, E. 1995. "The Politics of Privilege and Resistance." Pp. 91–97 in *Women, Culture, and Universities: A Chilly Climate?*, ed. A. M. Payne and L. Shoemark. Sydney: University of Technology, Sydney Women's Forum.

Rifkin, J. 1995. *The End of Work: The Decline of the Global Labor Force and the Dawn of the Post Market Era.* New York: G. P. Putnam's Sons.

Rizvi, F., and L. Walsh. 1998. "Difference, Globalization, and the Internationalization of Curriculum." *Australian Universities Review* 41:2:7–11.

R. M. I. T. University. 1997. *The Global University: A 21st Century View*, 2nd International Conference. Melbourne: R. M. I. T. University.

Roberts, A. 2000. "Introduction: Launching the Opposition." Pp. 10–12 in *Burning Down the House: The Bonfire of the Universities*, ed. P. James. Melbourne: Association for the Public University, with Arena Publications.

Sassen, S. 1996. "Toward a Feminist Analysis of the Global Economy." *Indiana Journal of Global Legal Studies* 4:1:7–25.

Seddon, T. 1999. "Research Recommendations and Realpolitik: Consolidating the Ed.D." *The Australian Educational Researcher* 26:3:1–15.

Sharp, G., and D. White. 1968. "Features of the Intellectually Trained." *Arena* 15:30–33.

Simeone, A. 1987. *Academic Women: Working Towards Equality.* South Hedley, Mass.: Bergin & Garvey.

Smith, T., ed. 1996. *Ideas of the University, Research, Research Institute for the Humanities and Social Sciences.* Sydney: University of Sydney, with Power Publications.

Stewart, T. A. 1997. *Intellectual Capital: The New Wealth of Organizations.* London: Nicholas Brealey.

Weber, S. 1996. "The Future of the University: The Cutting Edge." Pp. 43–77 in *Ideas of the University, Research, Research Institute for the Humanities, and Social Sciences*, ed. T. Smith. Sydney: University of Sydney, with Power Publications.

Watts, R. 2000. "A Circus Run by Clowns." Pp. 25–32 in *Burning Down the House: The Bonfire of the Universities*, ed. P. James. Melbourne: Association for the Public University, with Arena Publications.

Wells, J. 2000a. "Privatization by Stealth? Senate Committee to Review ARC Legislation." In *Advocate*, Journal of the National Tertiary Education Union 7:5:11.

Wells, J. 2000b. "Photocopying the Green Paper." Pp. 46–51 in *Burning Down the House: the Bonfire of the Universities*, ed. P. James. Melbourne: Association for the Public University, with Arena Publications.

# CHAPTER EIGHT

# CONCLUDING THOUGHTS ABOUT
# ENTREPRENEURSHIP AND CROSSING BORDERS

---

Deborah Mindorff and Cecilia Reynolds

*Canada*

The women whose work is showcased in this book are scholars and practitioners in the field of educational administration. They have taught and undertaken research in a variety of school settings, and they have taken on numerous administrative roles. Throughout the dialogue of this book, the authors have built "joint frames of reference"(Edwards and Mercer 1987, 65) that help readers consider and possibly revise their vision of school leadership. Readers are encouraged to clarify the origins of their perspectives regarding women as school leaders. They are challenged to look beyond traditional definitions, perceptions, and assumptions about women and men as leaders and to consider new and alternative perspectives.

In this final chapter, we look back across the book to consider two major themes that suggest some alternative perspectives on leadership—crossing borders and women as entrepreneurs in different contexts.

## CROSSING BORDERS

In an international book such as this, there is a heightened sensitivity to the importance of context. Reading about school leaders in different countries, however, also calls into question aspects of even our most familiar contexts. Dressel suggests that it is important to ask ourselves and others the questions: "How do you know?" or "What makes you think that?" (cited in Morgan and

Saxton 1994, 96). Another way to understand alternative perspectives is to make the strange familiar and the familiar strange (Erickson 1973). Glesne and Peshkin (1992) suggest:

> To make the familiar strange is often more difficult, because you must con-
> tinually question your own assumptions and perceptions, asking yourself:
> Why is it this way and not different? Overcome your disposition to settle
> into a way of seeing and understanding that gives you the comfort of clo-
> sure at the price of shutting down thought. (42)

This advice can be very relevant when considering a recurring theme in this book, the notion of crossing borders. One of the first borders we may need to cross as we consider women and school leadership is the one we confront when we need to rethink our comfortable perspectives. If we con-sider this an actual border crossing, we become more cognizant of the importance of looking at where we have come from in order to understand where we are going.

When we travel out of our own country, for example, we do so with an understanding, or at least a recognition, of the differences and similarities of the new territory we are entering. We are responsible to that new country's laws and socially responsible to its culture and customs. We make efforts to make sense of another way of thinking, another way of doing, and often another way of acting. Our efforts are compounded if learning moves beyond the cognitive to a level where we actually begin to feel and identify with the individuals of that new country. This often is the case when someone moves to a new coun-try for a prolonged stay. Things that may have seemed unusual as a visitor now take on a new meaning as a resident.

It also is important to recognize that there can be more than one route used to cross an actual border. The route we choose to take (given that we have a choice) may not be the fastest or the most direct, but it can lead to the same destination. Every traveler makes decisions based on the information, resources, and allotted time for travel he or she has available at that moment.

This book addresses a number of border crossings made by women in school leadership. Each chapter can be thought of as a route or road. Using that analogy, Hall in chapter 1 could be described as talking about the pros and cons of collecting tolls along a road. Her suggestion that we rethink entrepre-neurship in education can be seen as a reality statement about the real costs associated with taking up leadership roles in education. There is a cost involved, and somehow, somewhere, and at sometime we must ask, "Who will pay that cost? Can we really expect quality educational leadership, like we might expect quality roads, without paying a 'toll'? Would we be willing to accept alternatives?"

Hall asks us to rethink entrepreneurship as a road in educational leader-ship. She recognizes it as a road with a toll, which may or may not be a good thing. Her recommendation is that we always ask the following questions: "In whose interest has this 'road' been built?" "What is the price we must pay for traveling on this road?"

Reynolds, in the next chapter, considers over generations the main people involved in the construction of "roads." She looks at the broader picture, the macro-environment, and she draws our attention to the historic influences pushing the development of certain roads over others. She suggests how these may have limited the availability of choices for those who followed later and how these may have impacted the decision-making process of individual men and women in school leadership roles.

Elements of the remaining chapters fit this road metaphor as well. Blackmore makes us aware of signage along the route. Young draws our attention to road statistics such as who the drivers and passengers are and how many vehicles are traveling on the road. Schmuck, Hollingsworth, and Lock discuss potential roadblocks and alert us to some of the collisions that have happened. Strachan arouses our interest in those drivers who dare to make their own route and venture off of the beaten path. Kenway and Langmead are like helicopter traffic reporters in that they give an overview of the present situation while humorously describing what may be in store for travelers on the road ahead. One of the things that may be ahead is the need for women and men in schools to rethink what it means to be an entrepreneur in a school setting.

## WOMEN AS ENTREPRENEURS IN DIFFERENT CONTEXTS

In the final words of her opening chapter, Hall challenges readers to "take account of the positive lessons we learn from women in these positions and consider how they can be combined with a greater awareness of what is needed to create social justice." Her words stress how we can learn from the experiences of others. The focus of Hall's chapter is to reexamine the contrasting interpretations of entrepreneurial activity and to encourage women leaders to translate those elements that promote social justice and equality into education. Hall challenges us to be "reinterpreting entrepreneurship" in education in such a way as to make it compatible "with education's moral purpose."

There is an associated misconception that goes with the term *entrepreneurship*, because the word has undergone radical historical development. In the past, it used to have a very negative connotation, because it was closely associated with exploiting people or radicalizing whole economies. Today, however, the term has taken on a more positive meaning, one that symbolizes the attributes of exploiting opportunities rather than people.

Sexton and Bowman-Upton (1991) provide a list of terms used to describe entrepreneurs historically and presently. In the same way there are alternative versions of "feminisms" presented in this book, there also are many versions of "entrepreneurship" evident in the existing scholarly literature.

Often entrepreneurship is narrowly conceived of as being associated only with business enterprise or new venture development rather than denoting the characteristics of a person who has an enterprising attitude or a creative spirit. The concept of capitalizing on an entrepreneurial mind-set within an educational setting is gaining wider acceptance. In Sweden, Andersson (1992) uses this broader understanding of entrepreneurship to describe an entrepreneurial school as one that includes "initiative, curiosity, joy in discovering, creative experimenting in reality, reflections on experiences, and a constant search for challenges" (Andersson 1992, 16).

One way to look at entrepreneurship within an educational setting particularly relevant to this book is taken from the report *Towards an Enterprising Culture—A Challenge for Education and Training* (CERI 1989), "an ability to act and to pursue a task (specifically in a new manner or outside established borders)" (Andersson 1992, 16).

Another meaning of enterprise that is especially relevant to leaders in education is provided from a private, nonprofit organization that describes it as "taking initiative to achieve a self-determined goal that is part of a future vision, in order to achieve one's own meaning in life, while sharing achievements with others" (Wilson and Mindorff 1999).

Based on this definition, the Institute for Enterprise Education in Ontario, Canada, cooperated in a partnership with the Faculty of Education at Brock University, Canada, to develop a new education program called "Bachelor of Education in Enterprise Education." The program is intended to develop teachers' capabilities for the twenty-first century by helping preservice teachers develop an enterprising approach to their work as teachers in the community.

It is clear that the notion of "entrepreneurship" is controversial, even within this book. However, a fruitful road can be followed by considering social entrepreneurship. The social entrepreneur is described by Morato (1994) in this way:

> Social entrepreneurs may employ social, economic, political, or even ecological interventions to pursue their altruistic objectives. Thus, enterprise establishment is not the only means available to the social entrepreneur. The social entrepreneur may organize communities, educate them, raise their awareness levels, increase their capacity to manage themselves, and motivate them to start making claims on the government or on society, in order to improve their economic well-being, raise their social status and standards of living, and increase their political power. (2–3)

One view of the social entrepreneur is that he or she sets out deliberately to use his or her entrepreneurial talents to "promote the successful creation of enterprises or livelihood endeavors for those in need" (Morato 1994, 2). In his view, Morato suggests that social entrepreneurs have only one distinct difference from other entrepreneurs, that is, that they help others to prosper. Examples are given by Morato of social enterprises that can be in the form of cooperatives, livelihood associations, or even organized communities. These can exist as corporations, institutions, foundations, organizations, or temporary committees for the purpose of some common goal whereby the less privileged or poorer segments of society are uplifted. The social entrepreneur may achieve a set financial or physical goal, or may simply act in raising the awareness, or the capacity level, of a particular group.

It is interesting to see the way in which two successful entrepreneurial women have expanded the role of an "entrepreneurial educator" toward worthy projects of social entrepreneurship in the Republic of the Philippines. One example is of a female political leader who explained the challenges she encountered with the "old boys club," especially with regard to graft and bribery in handing out provincial construction projects in her region:

> I was determined not to fall into the "old boys club" game. Yet I knew that my region desperately needed roads built, if we were to stimulate our local economy. It seemed I could not get around the corruption of the construction process. I was in political office. What did I know about construction? So I reversed the situation and put a construction company into the political office. We purchased our own heavy equipment, hired our own local people, as supervisors and labourers, and bought our materials locally. The roads got built, our own people were empowered, and I completely avoided any entanglement with the "old boys club." (Mindorff 1997/1998)

Another woman who had risen to one of the highest executive positions for a major Filipino corporation took on a dual role as an entrepreneur and a change agent in Philippine society when she left her established position in the corporate world and went to work for herself. She commented:

> There is a feeling that you simply cannot describe when you are able to see change in someone's life because of your actions. The thirty-five women who started with me only had rags to wear, they were very poor when I gave them work. I trained them all myself, even though people said I was making a mistake. I taught them how to do things, I gave them skills they did not have before. You would not believe these are the same women. Today they have pride in their work and more importantly, in themselves. (Mindorff 1997/1998)

In these situations some might say that "necessity was the mother of invention," however, it is clear from both of these women's comments that despite entrenched barriers to change, they were able to combine the resourcefulness and resiliency of an entrepreneurial spirit to bring about social and educational change.

Reconsidering entreperneurship is not the only challenge put forth by the authors in this book. Another important theme is understanding the importance of contexts with regard to women leaders in education. Each of the authors has utilized a different approach to do this. Taken together, the chapters allow for comparisons across divergent contexts, including different time periods and cultures.

One useful way to think about the chapters is to consider the different types of comparisons the authors have used, or what Neuman (1997) calls equivalence. Neuman describes four distinct types, including conceptual, contextual, lexicon, and measurement equivalence (409–12), and each type can be identified in the chapters in this book.

Hall (chapter 1) provides a narrative of her own journey as an educational leader that she uses as a springboard to contrast research findings from two different sectors, business and education, as well as different cultures and countries. She uses a conceptual equivalence based on her experience and knowledge from her own culture and era, which she is then able to relate to other research.

Reynolds (chapter 2) puts historical time at the center of her research and "treats what is studied as part of the flow of history and situated in a cultural context" (Neuman 1997, 382). Reynolds thus uses contextual equivalence in her historical study by including men and women in her research of principalships. This approach provides a richer context of what was going on during that time period and a fuller understanding of the perspectives of both men and women. This method of inquiry is more holistic, as it goes beyond criticisms of androcentrism or feminocentrism (the practice of viewing the world and shaping reality from a male lens then, conversely, from a female lens) (Shakeshaft 1987; Warren 1988). Reynolds tries to understand gender issues within a more complete social context.

Blackmore (chapter 3) considers the various scripts of women within the historical development of the new managerialist context and demonstrates the importance of lexicon (language) equivalence, which Neuman (1997) describes as the proper translation of words or finding an equivalent alternative for that word (411). Her chapter demonstrates the importance of changes in scripts and in the meanings of words over time.

In Young's (chapter 4) research, statistical data and the way in which statistical information is gathered are scrutinized. Young employs measurement equivalence and illustrates why it becomes extremely difficult to conduct any type of quantitative cross-country or cross-cultural data analysis when there are differences in terminology and methods of collecting statistical data. Caution is recommended in cross-cultural research. Young's description of the difficulties she encountered when "cutbacks" affected the availability of longitudinal databases should be a warning that information should continue to be collected in such a way that gender analysis is possible. This often is a prerequisite in the international arena of foreign aid. The Canadian International Development Agency (CIDA) and other larger developmental agencies frequently mandate that gender statistics be kept in the developing countries where they are providing assistance. Curiously, Young's work suggests that this is not always done within Canada. This may come as a great surprise to many men and women who assume that with equal opportunity and affirmative action programs gender data are being collected as a matter of course.

Some readers also may have been surprised somewhat by the data presented in the case studies outlined by Schmuck, Hollingsworth, and Lock (chapter 5) and Strachan (chapter 6). These authors have used both contextual and lexicon equivalencies in their work. In chapter 7, by Kenway and Langmead, all four of Neuman's equivalences are put to use to argue for a call to action by school leaders in light of clear and present dangers presented by the new form of "governmentality" in many of today's universities.

Kenway and Langmead remind us that rethinking the very design of an organization is perhaps one of a leader's most important tasks. Senge (1990) quotes a leader in his study who states: "We need a new generation of organizational architects. . . . Most changes in organizational structure are piecemeal reactions to problems. Real designers are continually trying to understand wholes" (343).

This book urges us to become such organizational architects. We need to consider that as we endeavor to become more reflective leaders, we may need to cross a number of socially constructed borders. Schein (1993) suggests that, "What we perceive is often based on our needs, our expectations, our projections, and most of all, our culturally learned assumptions and categories of thought" (46). Whether you are male or female, an academic administrator, a teacher, a researcher, or a student, this book urges you to reflect critically on the existing literature on school leadership. Many of the assumptions that underpin that literature and the categories of thought that are employed fail to encompass the experiences of women leaders or the need to promote equity and social justice. This book encourages you to think about what your contribution will be to the empowerment of women as educational leaders in the new millennium. Berlak and Berlak (1987) explain:

> Empowerment implies contributing to the shaping of society, rather than being subjected to the powers of others. It goes beyond critical thought and includes a readiness to act with others to bring about the social conditions that one has chosen through a process of collaborative, critical inquiry. Action requires courage, but it also requires a possession of knowledge and skills necessary to change the situation—a classroom, school, or any other area of human activity. (170)

One of the strong elements of this book is the overt connection between ideas and actions, between shaping and being shaped. There is a recurring connection between ideas about the transformative learning process (Mezirow

1990) and the practices of transformative leadership by women educators (Kanter 1983; Owens 1998). This book demonstrates that transformative leadership is practiced by individuals who are eager and willing to participate in lifelong transformative learning. The insights provided by the text are both thought provoking and useful for researchers and practitioners because, as Owens (1998) states,

> only by knowing the contributions of those who came before us, those who pioneered in building the knowledge that we have for thinking about organizations and leadership, can you prepare yourself to make the strategic and tactical decisions that will undergird your leadership with steadfast purpose, consistency, and effectiveness. (4)

## REFERENCES

Andersson, S. 1992. "The Entrepreneurial School." *Wingspan* 12:2–16.

Berlak, A., and H. Berlak. 1987. "Teachers Working with Teachers to Transform Schools." Pp.169–78 in *Education Teachers: Changing the Nature of Pedagogical Knowledge*, ed. J. Smyth. Lewes: Falmer Press.

CERI. 1989. "Towards an Enterprising Culture—A Challenge for Education and Training." *OECD/CERI.* Paris: Mimeo.

Edwards, D., and N. Mercer. 1987. *Common Knowledge: The Development of Understanding in the Classroom.* London: Methuen.

Erickson, F. 1973. "What Makes School Ethnography 'Ethnographic?'" *Council on Anthropology and Education Newsletter* 4:2:10–19.

Glesne, C., and A. Peshkin. 1992. *Becoming Qualitative Researchers: An Introduction.* New York: Longman.

Kanter, R. M. 1983. *The Change Masters: Innovation and Entrepreneurship in the American Corporation.* New York: Simon & Schuster.

Mezirow, J. 1990. "Toward transformative learning and emancipatory education." Pp. 251–69 in *Fostering Critical Reflection in Adulthood: A Guide to Transformative and Emancipatory Learning*, ed. J. Mezirow and Associates. San Francisco: Jossey-Bass.

Mindorff, D. 1997/1998. Unpublished interviews with female political leaders in the Republic of the Philippines.

Morato, E. A., Jr., 1994. *Social Entrepreneurship and Enterprise Development.* Manila, Philippines: Asian Institute of Management.

Morgan, N., and J. Saxton. 1994. *Asking Better Questions: Models, Techniques, and Classroom Activities for Engaging Students in Learning.* Markham, Ontario: Pembroke.

Neuman, W. L. 1997. *Social Research Methods: Qualitative and Quantitative Approaches.* Needham Heights, Mass.: Allyn & Bacon.

Owens, R. G. 1998. *Organizational Behavior in Education*, 5th ed. Boston: Allyn & Bacon.

Schein, E. H. 1993. "On Dialogue, Culture, and Organizational Learning." *Organizational Dynamics* 22:2:40–51.

Senge, P. 1990. *The Fifth Discipline: The Art and Practice of the Learning Organization*. New York: Bantam Doubleday, Dell Publishing Group.

Sexton, D.L., and N. B. Bowman-Upton. 1991. *Entrepreneurship: Creativity and Growth*. New York: Macmillan.

Shakeshaft, C. 1987. *Women in Educational Administration*. Newbury Park, Calif.: Sage.

Warren, C. 1988. *Gender Issues in Field Research*. Newbury Park, Calif.: Sage.

Wilson, S., and D. Mindorff. 1999. *Final Report of the Enterprise Education/Teacher Education Program*, Brock University, Ontario, Canada.

# About the Contributors

JILL BLACKMORE is an Associate Professor, School of Social and Cultural Studies, Faculty of Education, Deakin University, Australia. She has researched and published on organizational change, leadership, globalization, educational restructuring, teachers' work, school governance, gender equity reform, the parental movement, and citizenship education. She has co-edited *Gender Matters in Educational Administration and Policy: A Feminist Introduction* with Jane Kenway and has co-authored with Jane Kenway, Sue Willis, and Leonie Rennie in *Answering Back: Girls, Boys, Education, and Feminism*. She is the author of *Troubling Women: Feminism, Leadership, and Educational Change*.

VALERIE HALL is a Reader at the University of Bristol, United Kingdom. She has researched and published on a wide range of issues related to managing people in education. Her work has focused on professional development, adult learning, team leadership, and equal opportunities. She is the author of *Dancing on the Ceiling: A Study of Women Managers in Education*.

SANDRA (SAM) HOLLINGSWORTH is a Professor of Teacher Education at San Jose State University—the third of her academic homes. A former historian and classroom teacher, she took her first academic position at the University of California, Berkeley. There she conducted longitudinal research on the impact of teacher education coursework on beginning teachers in urban schools. Beginning in 1990 at Michigan State University, she worked on professional development school arrangements in Michigan and Asia. Using the inquiry process of action research, she has published four books on topics including urban partnerships in education, the praxis of "multiple literacies," and international social studies. She continues to conduct research on the longitudinal effects of her own teaching.

JANE KENWAY works as a Research Professor at the University of South Australia. Her research expertise is in education policy and sociology with reference to schools and educational systems in the context of wider social and cultural change. Her specific research interests include justice, vocational education in changing technological contexts, globalization, marketing education, and gender reforms in schools. She has published widely in journals and books for the education profession. Recent books include *Answering Back: Girls, Boys, Education, and Feminism* and *Consuming Children: Entertainment, Advertising, and Education* (forthcoming), with Elizabeth Bullen.

DIANNA LANGMEAD works as a Researcher at the Deakin Center for Education and Change at Deakin University, Australia. She has been actively involved in the women's movement, the community, and the university. Her research interests center around women, work, and education. Recent areas of research include the effects of marketization and globalization on education, gender and educational performance, critical literacy and English as a second language, and youth and citizenship. She currently is a graduate student at Deakin.

ROBYN LOCK is currently appointed in the Kinesiology Department at San Francisco State University. She has previous experience at San Jose State University and the University of Toledo, Ohio. In her thirty years as an educator, she has served as a public school physical education teacher, a high school and an intercollegiate coach, an athletic director, and a teacher educator. She has authored numerous articles on gender equity and other feminist issues in physical education and sports.

DEBORAH MINDORFF is a Research Officer in the Faculty of Education at Brock University, Canada. She recently completed a graduate program there. Her research focused on adult education, transformative learning, entrepreneurship, enterprise education, women in development, and community and international sustainable development. She is planning on pursuing her doctoral studies. She also worked as an editorial assistant on this book.

CECILIA REYNOLDS is Associate Professor and Associate Dean, Academic Program at the Ontario Institute for Studies in Education of the University of Toronto, Canada. Previously she was Director of Women's Studies and then Chair of the Graduate Program in the Faculty of Education at Brock University. An elementary and secondary classroom teacher for seventeen years, her research has focused on gender and power in school organizations, single-sex schools, cross-generational studies, and sustainable development in international contexts. She has contributed to numerous education and women's studies journals and edited collections and is co-editor, with Beth Young, of *Women and Leadership in Canadian Education*. She also is the editor of this book.

PATRICIA SCHMUCK is Professor and Chair of the Department of Educational Administration at Lewis and Clark College, Portland, Oregon. She has authored numerous books and articles about women and educational administration. These include *Women As Educators, Group Processes in the Classroom*, with Richard Schmuck, and *Gender Consciousness and Privilege: A Case Study of Single Sex and Coeducational Catholic High Schools* (forthcoming). She also has edited *Women Leading in Education*, with Diane Dunlap. She is actively engaged in consultancy work and is currently developing an Ed.D. program at Lewis and Clark College.

JANE STRACHAN is Assistant Dean of Graduate Studies in the School of Education at the University of Waikato, New Zealand. She taught as a high school teacher for twenty-two years. She now teaches in the masters and doctoral program in educational leadership. Her particular teaching and research interests are in the area of educational leadership and social justice and qualitative research methodologies. She has been published in both local and international journals, including *School Organization* and *Gender and Education*. Her most recent publication in the *Journal of Educational Administration* won a citation for excellence.

BETH YOUNG is a Professor in the Department of Educational Policy Studies at the University of Alberta, Canada, where she completed her Ph.D. in educational administration. Her research and publications relate primarily to gender issues in Canadian educational administration and policy, focusing on women educators' careers and on a feminist critique of our existing knowledge base. Most recently, she has been exploring part-time teaching arrangements and experiences. Her work has been published in journals and edited collections, and she is co-editor, with Cecilia Reynolds, of *Women and Leadership in Canadian Education*.

# FURTHER READING

Acker, S. 1999. *The Realities of Teachers' Work: Never a Dull Moment*. London and New York: Cassell.

Ah Nee-Benham, Maenettc, and Joanne Cooper. 1998. *Let My Spirits Soar: Narratives of Diverse Women in School Leadership*. Thousand Oaks, Calif.: Corwin.

Avolio, J. Bruce. 1999. *Full Leadership Development*. Thousand Oaks, Calif.: Sage.

Bacchi, Carole Lee. 1999. *Women, Policy, and Politics*. London and Thousand Oaks, Calif.: Sage.

Bailey McGee, Susan. 1992a. *Girls in Schools*. Wellesley, Mass.: Wellesley Centers for Women.

Bailey McGee, Susan. 1992b. *How Schools Shortchange Girls*. Wellesley, Mass.: Wellesley Centers for Women.

Bailey McGee, Susan. 1992c. *The Status of Girls in the U.S. Educational System*. Wellesley, Mass.: Wellesley Centers for Women.

Bank, J. Barbara, and M. Peter Hall. 1997. *Gender, Equity, and Schooling*. New York: Garland.

Betters-Reed, L. Bonita. 1993. *The Whitewash Glass Ceiling: Differences among Managerial Women of Color and White Women*. Wellesley, Mass.: Wellesley Centers for Women.

Bhopal, Kalwant. 1997. *Gender, "Race," and Patriarchy*. Aldershot, Hants, England and Brookfield, Vt.: Ashgate.

Blackmore, J. 1999. *Troubling Women: Feminism, Leadership, and Educational Change*. Buckingham: Open University Press.

Blount, J. M. 1998. *Destined to Rule the Schools: Women and the Superintendency 1873–1995*. Albany: State University of New York Press.

Brunner, C. Cryss, ed. 1999. *Sacred Dreams: Women and the Superintendency*. Albany: State University of New York Press.

Clinchy E., ed. 1997. *Transforming Public Education.* New York: Teachers College Press.

Cohee, E. Gail. 1998. *The Feminist Teacher Anthology.* New York: Teachers College Press.

Collette, Christina, and Fiona Montgomery, eds. 1997. *Into the Melting Pot.* Aldershot, Hants, England and Brookfield, Vt.: Ashgate.

Crosby, C. Barbara. 1999. *Leadership for Global Citizenship.* Thousand Oaks, Calif.: Sage.

Dunlap, D., and P. Schmuck, eds. 1995. *Women Leading in Education.* Albany: State University of New York Press.

Eaton, C. Susan. 1994. *Women and Union Leadership in U.S. and Canada: A Comparison.* Wellesley, Mass.: Wellesley Centers for Women.

Edwards, Julia. 1995. *Local Government Women's Committees.* Aldershot, Avebury, England: Ashgate.

Ferree, Marx Myra, ed. 1998. *Revisioning Gender.* Thousand Oaks, Calif.: Sage.

Fullan, Michael, and Andy Hargreaves. 1996. *What's Worth Fighting For?* New York: Teachers College Press.

Greene, Maxine. 1988. *The Dialectic of Freedom.* New York: Teachers College Press.

Hall, Peter. 1997. *Race, Ethnicity, and Multiculturalism.* New York: Garland.

Hall, Valerie. 1996. *Dancing on the Ceiling: A Study of Women Managers in Education.* London: Routledge.

Judge, Q. William. 1999. *The Leader's Shadow.* Thousand Oaks, Calif.: Sage.

King, E. Joyce, ed. 1997. *Preparing Teachers for Cultural Diversity.* New York: Teachers College Press.

Lambert, Linda. 1995. *The Constructivist Leader.* New York: Teachers College Press.

Littrell, Mary Anne. 1999. *Social Responsibilities in the Global Market.* Thousand Oaks, Calif.: Sage.

Martens, Lydia. 1997. *Exclusion and Inclusion.* Brookfield, Vt.: Ashgate.

Maschke, J. Karen. 1989. *Educational Equity.* New York: Garland.

Powell, N. Gary, ed. 1999. *Handbook of Gender and Work.* Thousand Oaks, Calif.: Sage.

Quina, Kathryn. 1986. *Teaching Research Methods: A Multidimensional Feminist Curricular Transformation Plan.* Wellesley, Mass.: Wellesley Centers for Women.

Reynolds, C., and B. Young, eds. 1995. *Women and Leadership in a Canadian Context.* Calgary: Temeron Books (Detselig).

Russell, Julia. 1995. *A Question of Leadership in Changing Schools: Exploring the Gender Issues.* Wellesley, Mass.: Wellesley Centers for Women.

Star, Jennifer, and Marcia Yudkin. 1996. *Women Entrepreneurs: A Review of the Current Research.* Wellesley, Mass.: Wellesley Centers for Women.

Wells, J. Sandra. 1994. *Women Entrepreneurs.* New York: Garland.

# INDEX